The **RYA** Book of
Buying Your First
Sailing Cruiser

Second Edition

Malcolm McKeag

ADLARD COLES NAUTICAL • LONDON

Published by Adlard Coles Nautical
an imprint of A & C Black Publishers Ltd
37 Soho Square, London W1D 3QZ
www.adlardcoles.com

First edition 1999
Second edition 2004

ISBN 0-7136-6872-5

A CIP catalogue record for this book is available from the British Library.

A & C Black uses paper produced with elemental chlorine-free pulp, harvested from managed sustainable forests.

Typeset in 9.5 on 12pt Concorde Regular
Printed and bound in Singapore by Tien Wah Press

Note: While all reasonable care has been taken in the publication of this book, the publisher takes no responsibility for the use of the methods or products described in the book.

Contents

Foreword

'To be happy for a night, get drunk; to be happy for a month, get married; to be happy for life get a sailboat.'   Anon

For a well organised, well informed and careful person, owning a sailing cruiser and taking it to sea can be one of the greatest joys in the life of you and your family. For the disorganised, ill informed and careless person, owning the same boat can lead to tension, disaster, family stress, and even bankruptcy.

It is a constant source of wonder to the RYA Legal Department how many apparently rational, thoughtful and prudent people, who would not dream of buying a house or even a car without the most careful research and legal precautions, leave their common sense at home when they set out to buy a boat. Our files are a permanent reminder of the many potential ways in which the unwary can be separated from their money.

There is no doubt that buying a boat, particularly for the first time, but even for the experienced, can be a minefield. Should you buy new or secondhand? How to choose the right boat? Where to look? How much to pay? Whether to have a survey? Is the seller really the rightful owner or just a smooth talking con-man? Is there a hidden mortgage or other debt on the boat? How to raise the money? How to find the right insurance package? What equipment to buy? Where to find a mooring? Where to register? Most importantly of all, particularly for the novice, where to learn to sail safely, competently and enjoyably?

As a hugely experienced sailor in both racing and cruising yachts, who writes with a light touch and readable style, Malcolm McKeag is the ideal author to guide the aspiring boat owner though this minefield. His book is well researched, logically organised, interesting and amusing to read, and packed with that vital ingredient of common sense. Even the very first section of the first chapter 'Are you really sure about this this?' should stop the readers in their tracks to consider the many alternative ways of going sailing without actually having to buy and manage a boat.

Although there are few areas in boat ownership where an 'absolute guarantee' can be provided, I can safely say that any buyer who takes the time to read this book before looking for a boat, and takes careful account of the advice on each of the stages of choosing, buying and managing the boat, is unlikely to end up regretting the idea, and is even less likely to become immortalised in the RYA legal archives.

Edmund Whelan
RYA Legal Department

Introduction

There are few joys quite like owning your own small boat. Boat ownership is more than merely 'going sailing' – indeed to go sailing you might be better off not owning a boat at all. No, the pleasure of owning your own sailing cruiser has little to do at all with going sailing, and everything to do with sentiment, emotion, affection and a sense of, well – ownership.

Buying a sailing cruiser is probably the second biggest investment the average owner makes in his life. Even the most modest cruiser capable only of creek-crawling and sheltered coastal work is likely to cost several thousand pounds, while anything capable of going offshore is likely to cost tens of thousands. And yet for all the expense and risk involved, the legal side of buying a yacht can be as simple as buying a toy train set or a Wendy house for the garden for your child.

The Merchant Shipping Act defines a 'ship' as 'every description of vessel used in navigation'. Thus any yacht is a ship, even down to the smallest sailing dinghy or powerboat. By the same token, any yacht owned by a British National is a British ship, entitled to registration on one of the British shipping registers, and also to all the rights and liabilities attaching to registered British ships under the Merchant Shipping Acts and under international maritime law. Registration, however, is not compulsory – at least for craft under 12m.

Unlike a house, it is possible for a yacht to pass through many hands, from one owner to another, without ever being registered, without registration details being changed on each change of ownership or indeed without its existence, or that of the sale, ever being recorded. This is because a yacht is a chattel, rather than real property (like a house) and because registration is voluntary (unlike a motor vehicle where the Road Traffic Acts require every change of ownership to be notified to the Vehicle Licensing Authority). This absence of formality does not in any way imply that the buyer of a yacht does not obtain good title. But the contrast between, on the one hand, absence of formality and on the other the definition of a 'British ship', and all that it implies, gives considerable scope for the unwary to become ensnared in complication, either unwittingly or as the victims of less than honest dealing.

So, although a yacht can be bought and sold without formality and used without being registered, this is definitely not recommended. The purchase and use of a yacht is full of potentially expensive pitfalls for the uninitiated and experienced alike; the purpose of this book is to try and explain as many as possible of the related consequences of owning a sailing cruiser so that you, buying your first or even your second, third or fourth sailing cruiser, can identify those pitfalls and steer clear. We shall look at registration, insurance, checking title and raising money. We shall also help you to make the best choice of sailing cruiser and look at the places you can keep her and things you can do with her once you have found her.

Inevitably, some of the subjects sound dry and dusty. A hard look at potential pitfalls can too easily leave the impression that here is a world peopled by potential crooks, officious bureaucrats and avaricious sharks.

Be not afraid. The vast majority of people who buy a sailing cruiser get only pleasure and joy – even if it is the joy, as one experienced cruiser owner phrased it many years ago, 'of simply exchanging one set of worries for another'. But then, is it not a pleasure to have something as lovely as your own sailing cruiser to worry about?

1

What Sort of Sailing; What Sort of Cruiser?

Are you really sure about this?

Question: are you really sure you want to buy a boat at all? Many folk sail and cruise all their lives and never own the boats they sail in: they sail with friends. When you own your own cruiser, you will often seek the help of friends – to help you deliver the boat between family cruises, to bring the boat back when bad weather has stopped you getting home on your own, or simply for extra company. You could charter: if you work out the cost of boat ownership against hours spent sailing, charter is by a long way the cheaper option. You could join an organisation like the Island Cruising Club in Salcombe, Devon, where the club owns the boats and the members sail in them. Perhaps you might consider a flotilla holiday, where you can form your own group and together join an organised mini-fleet or a flotilla, or go as a single person or a couple and join others on a yacht in the flotilla. All of these ways of going cruising are infinitely cheaper than owning boats and, for those who do it, no less satisfying.

For some of us, though, there is just no substitute for owning our own boat – because boat ownership is so much more, so very much more, than merely sailing in it. For a start, when you own the boat, she ceases to be 'it'. She becomes 'she' – with all that that implies, irrespective of the owner's gender.

Before you buy, however, there are many questions to be asked – and the first is 'what sort of sailing do I (or we) intend to do in this boat?'

So many ways

There are almost as many ways to go sailing as there are boat owners, but there is no doubt that some boats are more suited for one sort of sailing than another. If you want to race, you probably do not want a solid, dependable, if a trifle unexciting, family cruiser. And if you want to go sailing with a young family, you almost certainly do not want a high-performance but tricky-to-sail racer or ex-racer. If you intend to sail primarily by yourself, you will want a smallish boat that is easy to sail – indeed that will sail herself – and that is rigged in such a way that the sail controls are kept as simple, and probably as few, as possible. If there are two of you plus three children, a simply-rigged boat, ideal for short-handed sailing, might well be thoroughly boring for all on board save one person. You are better off buying something that has lots of things to pull, to adjust, and play with.

If you live life to a busy and demanding schedule, your sailing cruiser must have a reliable and fairly powerful engine, to get you home at the appointed hour when the wind does not oblige. If it matters not when you get home; if you are one of those enviable people with the time and – just as important – the temperament to wait for time and tide, the size of the engine will probably not be as important as the scope for comfortable living aboard.

If you hate any sort of do-it-yourself work, you will not want a boat that will require intensive maintenance and upkeep; such a boat will soon become an albatross around your neck. Either you will dread going down to it, faced as you will be by all the jobs you need to do, or it will cost you a fortune paying someone else to do them for you. At the very least, the boat will end up looking like a badly-kept shed; at the worst, the improperly maintained boat will become a danger to you and your family. If, on the other hand, your idea of unalloyed joy is having an excuse to reach for your tools then an older boat – possibly wood – will bring you hours of pleasure without either of you even going near the water.

Where you live and where you will keep the boat is likewise an important factor in choosing the sort of boat you will buy. If you live in the middle of the country you are more or less inevitably faced with a long drive to the boat, no matter where you keep it. You might consider a trailer-sailer, if you have somewhere at or near home to keep her, or at least a boat you can bring nearer home during the off-season if you plan to do more than the simplest maintenance tasks yourself. If you buy a boat that is not easily road-transportable – and most boats are not – you will need carefully to plan your time and preparations each time you set out to visit her. You are probably also going to spend longer on each visit than someone who lives just round the corner from their boat – so you need a boat that is comfortable to stay aboard. You will probably end up paying someone else to do much of the work that owners who live close to their boats do themselves. Have you thought of moving house?

And of course, how much money you have to spend – both on the boat and on the pastime – will inevitably be a major factor in your plans.

Where do you want to sail?

Where you choose to sail – or for that matter where, perforce, you must sail – should greatly influence the sort of boat you look for. By the same token, where you choose to sail will be influenced by your level of experience. Estuary cruising and short-coast hopping are where most people begin, unless they happen to be Chay Blyth. (Chay – now Sir Chay – started his cruising with, by his own admission, little or no knowledge and decided to begin with a longish cruise: solo around the world, teaching himself navigation as he went. He bought a bilge-keel Kingfisher 22 and set off. He admitted that this was the wrong sort of boat for ocean cruising: wrong hull shape, wrong keel configuration, wrong rig, displacement too light, insufficient directional stability, to name but a few liabilities, which in a different boat could have been assets. His first voyage ended somewhere on the coast of Africa, not particularly gloriously. Chay's subsequent and more successful exploits at long distance sailing in rather more suitable yachts demonstrate to all of us the importance of the right choice of sailing cruiser.)

As we start to discuss 'horses for courses' we have to make something very plain – and then keep repeating it! It is a wise man or woman who, when asked to advise someone on what sort of boat they should buy, replies: 'I would no more advise you on your choice of boat than I would advise you on your choice of a wife or husband'. It is only with

(Opposite) *This Cornish Shrimper offers camping accommodation for two – and with its centreplate or lifting keel can get into those places bigger boats cannot reach. The active class association organises rallies, Old Gaffer meetings, even their own class in the Round the Island Race.*
Photo: David Harding

Spellbound, *the author's Hunter 701, is a typical first cruiser. Costing about £5,000 when she was new in 1973, this would cost about the same on today's second-hand market and will take you through several seasons before you have exhausted the possibilities she offers.* Photo: David Harding.

reluctance (and at the publisher's insistence) I venture into this area, for whatever guidelines one may offer there will always be someone who can prove them wrong, someone who – if I suggest you begin in a smallish boat – will be able to relate how their own first boat was close on 50ft (15m), weighed nigh on 20 tons, drew 7ft 6in (2.2m), had no engine and since the day they bought her they have never looked back. ('Just as well', someone else will remark, 'that they never looked back – to see the ranks of shaking fists, dismayed dockmasters and tangled lines that their first adventures left behind'.)

So let's say you agree that your early cruising is likely to be estuary sailing. Then it is likely you will want a fairly small boat. How small is small? Well – what age are you? 'A foot of waterline length for each year of age' is an old adage more honoured now in the breach than in the observance, and for

that matter not particularly realistic when first uttered by that arch old aphorist Uffa Fox – but the sentiment makes sense. As you get older, the inevitable minor discomforts, not to say rigours, of living aboard a small boat become magnified, while happily it is often the case that one has accumulated a little more wealth, and thus can afford a slightly larger boat.

For a first cruiser, 21ft (6.5m) is as small as I would advise anyone to select. Below that length, one is camping rather than cruising – an honourable and enjoyable enough pastime, but this book is about cruising. Straight away, we run into that problem about generalisation: *Shoal Waters* is a converted 16ft (4.8m) Fairey Falcon dinghy in which a splendid seafarer, the very doyen of estuarial cruisers, called Charles Stock has for many years cruised the coast and sandbanks, the rivers and creeks, the gullies and rills of the

East Coast of England. She was his first cruiser, is now his only cruiser and covers in excess of 1,000 miles a season. Charles and his wife, both now retired, appear to have no desire to get anything bigger. But Charles and his ilk, by any standard, are exceptions.

Draft is the next consideration – perhaps even more important than length. If you are going to be in and out of shallow harbours, up and down little creeks, you will limit yourself unnecessarily by choosing a boat that is too deep for the waters you cruise. Take a chart of the places you might like to cruise, check the depth of boat you are thinking of buying, draw a line around all the areas on the chart where you will not be able to float a boat of that draft at low water, shade them in and see how much of your chosen cruising ground you are going to miss. Many Thames Estuary sailors will agree that anything over 4ft (1.2m) draft is a bit of an embarrassment in that part of the world, while even in the West Country where the coast is steep-to and the main rivers deep enough to take sizeable ships, the upper reaches of the Helford, the Fal, the Dart and indeed most others are not ideal places to take deep-draft boats.

Perhaps the greatest boon of all to the estuary cruiser is the ability to vary draft with a centreboard or lifting keel. This way, one can have the best of both worlds: reasonable draft for good sailing performance, shallow draft for creek crawling or even merely for anchoring in the places deeper draft boats cannot get to, and thus avoiding the crowds. There are some very good variable draft designs, especially among older boats and on the second-hand market which, after all, is where most of us will find our first sailing cruiser.

Coast-hopping

Geographically, there is not a great deal of difference between estuary sailing and coastal cruising – indeed, if you have no estuaries near home you may be straight into coast-

hopping. Here, we better make the distinction that estuary cruising is in predominantly sheltered and semi-sheltered water where you should make your destination in a few hours; by coastal sailing we mean sailing in potentially unsheltered water, where the distances you cover may well keep you at sea overnight.

If you plan to coastal cruise your little ship must be sound and well-equipped enough to take bad weather, for you cannot guarantee you will not be caught out in a summer gale. By this I mean everything from a reliable auxiliary engine to navigation lights; from sails and sail systems that will allow you to reef or change sails easily to cockpit lockers and cabin doors that are secure and watertight; to having heavy items like batteries and anchors in secure stowage places where they will not get tossed around. All rigging, sails, equipment and, for that matter, hull and deck must be strong enough to get you out of trouble and should be checked often enough for wear and weakness so that when it comes on to blow you can be confident that nothing is going to break and leave you at the mercy of the sea.

Across the Channel

By which we mean, if you live on the South Coast of England, across the English Channel to France, or if you live on the East Coast, across the North Sea to Holland or Belgium. Or across to the Isle of Man, or Scotland, or Ireland. In other words, cruises where nights at sea are routine, and where, if it comes on to blow, you may find yourself plugging through it – or better still running before it – for hour after hour

Yet again, any attempt to generalise on the size or even type of boat will merely invite those who do it regularly in something different to prove us wrong. So perhaps the simplest advice is to get you to think what you are going to say to the lifeboat crew when they ask you:

'What in the name of Heaven are you doing out here in this?'

How much time do you have?

The amount of time you will devote to your cruising may also affect your choice, both of the sort of cruising you do and the boat you buy. This is really more a matter of how much time you will devote to your boat, rather than simply dictating the way in which you sail her. None of us who are still working have enough time for our cruising – but if time is really at a premium you will probably want the sort of boat where you can keep down-time to a minimum, and maximise your sailing time. Thus you will probably not want a boat that requires a great deal of maintenance – which rules out wood, and probably rules out the sort of boat owning where you do your own maintenance.

Also, if time for sailing is short, you really do not want to waste it sitting in the car on a motorway – so you will pick the sort of boat you can keep near home, perhaps even at home. Something trailable and fairly compact will mean estuary and river exploration rather than cross-Channel voyaging.

How experienced are you?

Even though this is your first sailing cruiser, you may already be an experienced sailor, perhaps in dinghies and small boats, perhaps a long-time racer who never before has had the time or inclination, or family reasons, or whatever, to think about going sailing for the mere joy of going sailing. Perhaps you have crewed for others before, but not owned your own boat, perhaps you have been on flotilla or sailing school holidays and reckon that by now you are sufficiently well-fledged to set out entirely on your own. If you have little or no experience, the soundest advice you can get might well be – don't buy your first sailing cruiser just yet. Get some time in – both for your own safety and peace of mind, and that of your family (especially if you take them with you).

Whatever your level of competence, the boat you buy should be within your capabilities. Buying a boat that is beyond you – whether too big, too light in displacement, too powerfully rigged or requiring too much work and upkeep – will quickly turn what should be an on-going pleasure and source of enjoyment into a nightmarish millstone round your neck which may end up frightening yourself and your family half to death!

What's out there?

As you start to turn the dream of owning your own sailing cruiser into a reality, one of the first things you are likely to do is start looking around to see what boats there are available. You will quickly discover there is a bewildering array of all sorts of craft – large, small, expensive, inexpensive. You may already know what sort of sailing you want to do, and will quickly disregard many. If you are still at the stage of wondering what sort of cruising is for you, looking at the boats on the market and asking yourself 'is this what we want?' is a good way of clarifying what you can undertake and afford.

There are a number of places to start gathering information about boats. If you live near a yachting centre, begin your search by driving around the boatyards and looking at what is for sale, either parked-up on the hard-standing or pictured on notice-boards and in brokers' windows. Going to boat shows is another way – although bear in mind that all you will see at major boat shows are new boats, at new boat prices. However, when the

(Opposite) *The great delight of the Southampton Boat Show each September is that many of the boats are on the water. It has a greater selection of smaller sailing cruisers than the more glitzy mid-winter London International Boat Show, while many of the nearby yards and marinas hold concurrent Used Boat shows.* Photo: David Harding.

Southampton International Boat Show is on each September, the boat yards at both Hamble and Lymington put on what they call Used Boat Shows; if you are in any way serious about this quest, both are worth a visit. At London International Boat Show, each January, most of the major brokers take stands, and there you can look at their lists and talk to them about what they have on their books.

The best place to look is probably in one or more of the yachting magazines which cater for a variety of markets and sailing styles. At the time of writing the classified sections of *Yachts and Yachting*, *Practical Boat Owner*, *Sailing Today*, *Yachting Monthly* or *Yachting World* would give a broad choice. This is not to denigrate any magazines not mentioned – merely to say that they tend to deal with other forms of sailing, and advertise other sorts of boats.

Yachts and Yachting is primarily a dinghy sailors' magazine with an exclusive emphasis on racing. However, it is the country's only fortnightly sailing magazine (all the others are monthlies) and has a large classified section – so private sellers of small sailing cruisers often use it because it can shift their boat quickly.

Practical Boat Owner and *Sailing Today* are both aimed very much at the sort of reader who might well be on the point of buying their first sailing cruiser, as well as readers who have previously owned their own little ships. They too have classified sections, but here also you will find the adverts of the brokers who handle the sort of boat you may be interested in.

Yachting Monthly has long called itself 'The Sea-going Magazine', and is exclusively devoted to cruising and cruising matters: its brokerage adverts are a must for anyone looking for their first sailing cruiser even though its advertisers offer boats well beyond the first time buyer. *Yachting World* also has a plethora of brokerage adverts – although here, it must be said, will be found more of the upper end of the market rather than the more modest boats that concern us.

Reading magazines and browsing the classified adverts will not only help you find your boat – it might well help you make up your mind on the sort of cruising you are going to do – which, as we have already agreed, is the decision which will define what sort of boat you should look for.

2

The Budget

The only thing about owning and running a sailing cruiser that is free is the wind that drives her. Everything else is going to cost money. This unpalatable truth has to be faced from the outset, for if it is not, then owning our boat is soon going to become a miserable experience – and probably a considerable source of friction between all those involved in her. That old saw about 'not being able to afford it if you have to ask how much it costs' owes more to wit than to common sense (and not a lot to wit, either). The good news is that the initial outlay need not be prohibitive. A small second-hand sailing cruiser can be purchased for the price of a reasonable second-hand car, and, with prudent management, its running costs need be little more. Of course, there are expensive boats, some of which can cost – new or second-hand – more than the vast majority of us pay for our houses. All things are relative. The important thing is to buy a boat that is within your means.

The costs of owning (as opposed merely to buying) a sailing cruiser break down into four broad categories: capital costs; unavoidable running costs; discretionary running costs; and associated use costs.

Capital costs

The obvious capital cost is that of the boat itself. We shall look at various ways in which you can 'raise the wind' (to use an old merchant-adventuring phrase meaning to finance your capital outlay) in a later chapter. However, the amount of capital you decide to invest and where it is coming from are inseparable parts of the same equation. You may decide to invest a windfall, allocate savings or divert some other investment, take out a loan and pay the capital cost out of income. How much of your own personal wealth, be it modest or great, you decide to invest in the boat can only be your decision. Some people have virtually all their worldly capital tied-up in their boat, sometimes to the extent of choosing to live in a more modest house than they otherwise could afford simply to have a bigger, better boat. There are a band of enthusiasts who invest all and make their boat their only home – but that is unlikely to be the choice of a first-time buyer and for them there are other books than this. Other people invest only a modest proportion of their discretionary capital in their boat.

More like a house than a car

However much you invest in the boat, it is wise – and indeed encouraging – to look on the investment more as you would the purchase of a house rather than a large consumable item such as a car. Cars have a steady, not to say alarming, rate of depreciation. In the normal course of events they are virtually worthless after a very short life – twenty years at most for most of them.

Boats last much longer, and relatively quickly the rate of depreciation approaches zero. Indeed in money, although, it cannot be too strongly emphasised, hardly ever in real terms, boats can actually appreciate in value. At its simplest, you as a buyer might pay for a second-hand boat about the same amount of money that the first owner paid for it when he bought it new. And when you come to sell, you could well get what you paid for it. You might, depending on what has happened to the economy, and the rate of inflation in the meantime, actually get more in money terms than you paid; this is particularly true if you buy a boat built before the dramatic oil price rises of the 1970s and the introduction of VAT.

It is important to remember we are talking in money values here, rather than in real terms. You will not (and should not expect to) get back when you sell what you have spent simply running the boat, nor are you likely to recover the cost of any extra gear – such as updated electronics – you might have put on board while you had her. Nor is it likely that your boat's value will keep pace with the apparently ever-rising cost of the same boat new, while you should also be aware that – just like investments on the stock market – the value of your boat can go down as well as up. And of course, if you pay too much for your boat in the first place you may well have difficulty finding someone also prepared to pay too much for it when you come to sell it.

Clearly there are exceptions to these very broad generalities. Some people seem always to be able to buy low and sell high, and occasionally – although rarely – someone who buys an old worn-out boat and does a magnificent restoration job actually sells the renovated boat at a substantial paper profit. However, the hours spent doing the restoration are not usually costed into the calculation.

After an initial post-showroom dip in value, boats may hold or even increase their money value, thus there is relatively little depreciation in real terms: broadly speaking the rate of depreciation should be about the same as the rate of inflation. Examination of the price of new boats seems, broadly, to reflect this view. For example, 30 years ago the cost of a new 32ft Contessa sailing cruiser was about £6,000, which was about the cost (unbelievable as it seems now) of a modest house. Today a Hunter Channel 31 costs about £60,000 (without the 17.5% VAT which did not exist 30 years ago) which is what the same house would cost today. Similarly, the Contessa cost what a luxury executive car would have cost 30 years ago – the Channel 31 costs what a luxury executive car costs today. (Even more interestingly, a second-hand Contessa 32 – if you can find one – costs today about £20,000, partly the result of the residual remains of the rampant inflation of the 1970s and 80s, partly a reflection of the high residual value of a well designed and built sailing cruiser.)

The same is largely true at the smaller end of the market: a 23-footer in 1972 cost around £4,000 or £5,000, or the price of a middle-market family car. Today, a 23-footer costs around £22,000 – still the price of a middle-market family car.

There is, however, one very important rider which must be attached to this cost business. Boats hold their value only when they are well looked after. A boat not properly looked after will deteriorate much more quickly than a car similarly ignored. If left afloat untended it will soon grow weed, its exterior finish will quickly dull; covers, if there are any, will be rotted as quickly by ultra-violet rays in sunlight as by rain, and blown and torn by wind. Water will get in and ruin upholstery and electronics alike; damp salt air will compound the mischief. The bilges will slowly fill. A couple of years of such neglect and the boat, if she is still afloat, will need a deal of money spent on her to bring her back up to any sort of usable, never mind saleable, condition.

Left ashore and similarly untended, the process of deterioration will merely be slowed. It will not be stopped.

The Hunter Channel, a tough performance cruiser, is above the budget end of the market, and will keep its value if well looked after. Available for home completion for those that way inclined.
Photo: David Harding.

Only a part of the story

The capital cost of the boat is but part of the budgeting story. Once you have bought her, there are the costs of keeping her. While circumstances inevitably alter cases and it is thus not possible to be too specific, we can say as a generalisation that you should expect the running costs of your boat to be, each year, somewhere around 10% to 15% of what you pay for her. If you buy second-hand, especially if you drive a very hard bargain, they may be as high as 20%.

Again, it is dangerous to over-generalise. The annual percentage figure will be higher, the lower the capital outlay, and vice versa: a £5,000 boat (yes, there are such unicorns still to be found) will almost certainly cost more than £500 a year to run; a £200,000 boat

need not cost £20,000 a year. Nonetheless, it is vital for the future of the project that at this stage you are honest with yourself in assessing not merely how much you can afford to spend on buying the boat, but how much you can afford to spend each year so that you may enjoy her. And for the sake of that enjoyment, you should let the latter figure determine what size and cost of boat you buy, rather than the former.

Unavoidable costs

Once you have bought your boat, there are some costs you will incur no matter what you do, where you keep her, or how you use her. One of these will be the cost of servicing the capital investment, whether it be the interest you are paying on the capital or the interest

11

you are losing by not having the capital invested elsewhere. There is also the cost simply of keeping her somewhere, ashore or afloat, even if you decide never to use her at all. You might be very lucky and own your own piece of waterside land where your boat can sit – but even if you pay yourself no rent for the right to keep your own boat there, such a cost (in this case zero) should be considered in your budget. Other unavoidable costs include insurance; essential main-tenance such as anti-fouling, if you keep the boat afloat, and the annual servicing of the engine; depreciation (and thus eventually replacement) of items such as sails, engine, running rigging; and the repair of inevitable breakages and small incidents of damage (hopefully all minor).

In Chapter 7 we look at the importance of careful assessment of the state of the boat when you are thinking of buying her, but this is a subject you should also consider when drafting your realistic budget. If you buy a new boat, there should be little need to make a budget allowance for replacement of essential parts for some years, but if you buy second-hand this could be a major consideration. The life of, for example, the engine is unlikely to be as long as the life of the well-looked after boat. Depending on the use and care (more often, lack of the latter) the engine life might be between 10 and 20 years. Even if the engine is sound, advances in design have meant that modern marine auxiliary engines are, size for size and weight for weight, much more compact and powerful (not to mention fuel-efficient and quiet) than their 20-year-old precursors. Re-engining a yacht is an expensive business, and you get no discounts just because you did not pay a lot for the yacht. It is, at 2003 prices, about a £7,000 job – whether your boat cost £16,000 or £46,000.

Similarly sails will need to be replaced regularly, and are an expensive item. It is not merely a matter of the performance of the boat. Old tired sails which detract from the performance of the boat will not only reduce your enjoyment in the craft you have bought, they may directly – and adversely – affect your safety and the safety of those with you. If the boat cannot sail well, you and she are less likely to be able to get out of difficulty. And if the sails are so old and tired they split and blow apart the first time you find yourself in a strong breeze, you are not likely to get into difficulty – you are already in it! A suit of basic working sails (mainsail and foresail) for a 27-footer will cost (2003 prices) about £3,000 to £5,000 – and again, you will get no discounts from the sail maker because you didn't pay much for the boat.

Discretionary running costs

Some items you can either do without altogether, or their purchase you can safely put off for another year. They include more or less all forms of electronic wizardry, for even such a fundamental item as a depth sounder comes into the category of desirable rather than essential. Also included are ancillary equipment such as cabin heaters; sails other than the basic working suit; outboard motors for the dinghy (and even the dinghy itself, for that matter); and so on – the list is as long as your pocket is deep. Yet although you might manage without them, some of these items can so enhance the scope of your sailing that their desirability borders closely on need. The boat you buy might have an old, very basic VHF radio set, for example, with limited range and without some or even many of the channels now commonly used. Almost certainly you will soon be telling yourself that you 'need' to replace it with a modern fully synchronised digital set. If your boat has an old GPS, no doubt you will soon similarly 'need' to upgrade to one with built-in chart software, of course. Such toys are all part and parcel of the pleasure of owning the principal toy herself.

(Opposite) *The Parker 235 is a trailer-sailer launched in 2002.*
Photo: David Harding

Associated costs of use

Virtually everywhere you go in the boat, you will incur some sort of charge for overnight parking. Unless you intend to sail resolutely throughout the day and night when you put to sea, or proceed direct to the remotest bays and coves of the coastline, the use of your boat – the indulgence of your pastime – will cost you money. This is what is meant by 'associated costs'.

Over many of these you can exercise some sort of choice. For example you might choose to raft up on the public visitors' berth on the Town Quay for £7.50 per night instead of paying £25.00 for your own berth in a marina where you have use of showers and similar facilities. You can choose to eat modestly on board rather than going ashore to patronise anything from the local pub and its grub to the swankiest of restaurants. You can drink home-made ale or the finest single malt. Nonetheless, owning and using your boat will incur some costs; happily these need be no more than you usually pay for your leisure activities, and will often turn out to be cheaper than other leisure pursuits.

The daily associated costs which go with a weekend's boating are much less than, for example, a ski-ing trip of similar duration, unless you get your ski-ing very cheaply and live very high on the hog when you go afloat. And if you have ever taken three children for a day at a theme park you will soon think family sailing a very sensible and cost-effective alternative.

There are some other associated costs you must take into consideration. If you do not already own a full complement of sailing gear, from foul-weather jacket and trousers, boots, safety harness and lifejacket to thermal underwear, smocks, casual tops and Breton-red sailing trousers, you will probably end up buying them, both for yourself and all who will regularly use the boat (unless the latter are of sufficient age and earning power to be told to go buy their own). You may decide to join a yacht club or a cruising association. You should include your subscriptions, along with your bar bill, when you first compile your 'can I afford it?' boat-owner's budget.

And of course you will become a personal member of the RYA, won't you?

3

Raising the Wind

Finding the money to buy your first sailing cruiser may, of course, be no problem. You might have it in the bank or building society already, and be ready when the time comes either to write a personal cheque, or withdraw a cheque from your building society account, made out in the name of the vendor or the broker from whom you are buying the boat.

Some vendors will try to insist on a delay long enough to allow the cheque to be cleared before handing over title, and with it the boat. While understandable in the case of a personal cheque drawn on a current account (the fear being there will be insufficient funds in the account to meet the cheque when it is presented) such a practice is entirely improper and quite unjustified. The reason it is not justified is that trying to buy something with a cheque the buyer knows will not be honoured is fraud, is a crime, and has its own remedies which are rather more dire than simply taking the boat back. Since (we assume) you are not attempting to commit a fraud as you buy your first sailing cruiser, you should insist on being given title to the boat when the cheque changes hands. Why should the vendor, however briefly, hold both the boat and your money? A vendor who is not prepared to trust you not to defraud him is a vendor upon whose own propriety you may care to ponder.

This difficulty can be overcome if you pay by banker's draft (but you will have to pay the bank a charge) or even by simple building society cheque. Such a cheque, which cannot be stopped (unless lost or stolen) and which, of course, is drawn against the funds of the building society, not an individual, is almost as good as cash.

Loans and mortgages

If you do not have – or do not wish to realise – the capital to buy the boat, you will need to borrow it. The two easiest ways to borrow are from a bank, or a specialist marine finance house – although in the past few years even credit card companies have been known to lend sums sufficiently large to buy even quite a sizeable small cruiser. Indeed there are now so many institutions pushing their willingness to lend us money down our e-mail or on to our doormats that it is wise to shop around.

Only you will know how much your bank manager will lend you on an unsecured loan – either a loan or an increase in your overdraft. If your cash shortfall is relatively modest – a couple of thousand pounds, say (although the real judgement is the amount you want to borrow relative to your income), it might well be worth a call to your bank manager before going down any more formal routes. The amount the bank will lend will depend on your income, what other irreducible outgoings the bank sees you have (house mortgage repayments, for example) and how quickly you will be able to pay off the debt.

In all these variables, it is the last-named which is the most likely to cut most ice. The shorter the term, the more likely the bank manager is to advance you the money. While the interest you will pay on such a loan will almost certainly be more than you will pay on a finance plan or marine mortgage, repayment arrangements will probably be easier and more flexible.

Such a loan, which you can re-pay at any time or in irregular instalments, may be more attractive to you than locking yourself into a less flexible finance plan or mortgage which may well have quite heavy financial penalties if you want to pay it off early. (To the lay borrower it always seems odd that someone already charging money to lend you funds would want to charge you even more if you think you'd like to pay them back earlier than you thought you might – but that's life among the city slickers.)

Loan or mortgage?

If the loan you need is less than about £15,000 or £20,000, it is likely that the finance house will not want to bother with the extra legalities involved but will instead offer a straightforward loan rather than a full-on mortgage, although the changes to the tax laws which come out of the Government Budget can suddenly alter the balance between the one and the other. Even if the boat itself is not the subject of a mortgage, the bank or finance house may expect some sort of security against such a loan: a second charge on your house mortgage, for example. The interest you will have to pay on such a secured loan will depend on the financial climate at the time, but in 2003 was about 4% above base rate.

If the amount you need is more than around £15,000, the finance house will probably want to take out a mortgage on the boat herself. Thanks to the security provided to the lender by the mortgage, the interest rate offered will probably be less than that charged on a straight loan, but the principal differences between a marine and a property mortgage is in the type of interest, and the term. Most marine mortgages are fixed-rate,

with the rate fixed at the time of the loan at a market figure something above base rate (in 2003, about 3% above). If the market changes, the term of the mortgage changes – lengthening for an increase, shortening for a decrease.

Unlike property mortgages where terms might be anything up to 50 years, marine mortgages are normally for terms of between 5 and 10 years: the cheaper the boat, the shorter the term. Again in contrast to property mortgages, the marine mortgage is usually for a smaller percentage of the total price, reflecting the fact that boats do not appreciate in value the way that houses do. The maximum loan you will be offered is unlikely to be more than 80%, but 50% is much more common.

If a mortgage is taken out on the boat, the finance house will wish to register the charge with the Registrar of Ships and Seamen, so that the boat cannot be sold or disposed of without the mortgage being redeemed. This is done via Part I Registration rather than the simpler Part III (Small Ships Register), and more on both forms of registration will be found in Chapter 10.

Stage payments

If you are buying new, the stage payments required by most builders (see Chapter 6) will of themselves offer a form of deferred payment, the instalments of which may well give you time and opportunity to raise the wind for your first sailing cruiser without having to go to a finance or mortgage house. Under most stage payment schemes, however, just who is lending money to whom is something of a moot point.

When thinking about how much you can afford, remember to include all the apparently extra, but in reality unavoidable, costs: from mooring fees to ancillary equipment like a dinghy, outboard and – for a second-hand boat – a reasonable provision for replacements and renewals. Photo: David Harding.

Shared ownership (partnership)

One way of easing the financial cost of your first sailing cruiser may well be to buy her as a joint enterprise with someone else. A great many sailing cruisers are very successfully operated by partnerships and syndicates – so the system can obviously work. However, it is also true that joint-ownership is a path littered with potential difficulties. These tend to arise in one (or more) of three specific areas: finding the right partner, operating the boat together, ending the partnership. In other words at every stage of the game – so it pays to consider the second two when thinking about the first.

Joining forces...

There is nothing that says a boat partnership has to be a marriage of equals, and indeed many of the most successful are not. Quite often, one partner provides most of the finance while the other, less in a position to do that, does most of the work. Or one partner brings to the deal knowledge and experience while the other has something equally weighty, but quite different to offer. What is important is that in this as in so many other partnerships, each party states clearly from the outset what is, and is not, expected.

... staying together...

There are as many ways of running a boat in partnership as there are of running a marriage, but a major difference is that one should not expect the boat partnership to be a 'til death do us part' arrangement. Many boat partnerships last for many years and indeed endure from boat to boat. Equally, many last for as long as it is convenient to all partners, and then end amicably. A very few turn out to be disasters, and end in tears. No matter what the future is to hold for the partnership, its dissolution should be planned for from the outset.

... coming apart

The biggest question is what is to happen to the boat when the partnership reaches the end of its natural life. If both partners agree to end the partnership, the solution is relatively simple: sell the boat and split the proceeds.

It is when one partner wants to pull out and the other to continue that the trickiest problem arises, and in such a circumstance it might be very sad for one to lose the boat he has come to love. If there is going to be a difficulty, it will probably arise when trying to agree what the boat is worth: the leaving partner clearly hopes the value of the boat will be as high as possible, the better to realise his capital investment; the staying partner, hoping to buy the other out, is moved to value the boat in terms of twice the amount which he feels is the minimum he can decently offer his friend. Even between friends this thorny question can strain things; if there is any acrimony in the reason for the split-up, you may be sure that facing all this for the first time at so late a stage will serve only to increase it.

The obvious way is to have the boat valued by an independent arbiter whose judgement both partners agree beforehand to accept. With the best will in the world, however, who is to say that this independent arbiter is right, or wrong? Look at the variety of asking prices for similar boats in the brokerage adverts, or indeed the prices the boats actually sell for – there is considerable variation. Ask two estate agents to value your house and nine times out of ten, each will give different figures. Why should boats be any different? At best, agreeing to let some independent 'expert' decide the value of the boat for such a purpose is to leave at least one of you, if not both, something of a hostage to fortune.

Sealed bids

One very neat solution, invented as far as I am aware by the Scottish yachting writer and well-known cruising sailor Michael Balmforth, is as follows. It is agreed from the

A bigger boat like this Moody 38 may require a bigger investment than planned for your very first sailing cruiser – but going into partnership perhaps even with someone who already owns part or all of the boat you are buying into, can give you the taste for ownership without over-committing yourself. Photo: Moody, Southampton.

beginning that if one partner wants out he has only to say so. If the other partner does not want to sell the boat and split the proceeds, he agrees he will offer the leaving partner a sealed bid. This sealed bid represents the figure the staying partner will pay the leaving partner to buy him out completely.

Now comes the clever bit: the leaving partner has the choice either to accept the bid or to reverse the deal and buy out the staying partner for the amount he himself has just been offered. The staying partner is obligated by the partnership agreement to sell to his partner for the same amount as he has offered to buy. The partnership is then dissolved with the leaving partner taking with him the boat, selling it and keeping the proceeds on the entire sale, having paid off the staying partner to the amount of the bid.

Picking the figure to put in the bid is a nice judgement for the staying partner, since he is agreeing to sell his share for exactly the same price as he is offering to pay – but it is certainly a good way of ensuring that the staying partner offers the leaving partner what he thinks is a fair price. In practice, unless there is some sort of acrimony, what is most likely to happen is that the bid figure will be discussed between all the partners before the actual bid is made, so everyone is happy.

Naturally, such an agreement should be incorporated in the partnership agreement you draw up together as you plan to buy the boat.

4

New or Second-hand?

There is an Irish yachtsman's saying: 'foolish men build boats for wise men to buy'. More prosaically, the British Marine Federation (BMF) estimate that between 70% and 80% of first-time buyers buy a second-hand boat. The figure encompasses all boats, including dinghies, but from it we may safely assume that many people buying their first sailing cruiser will be acquiring one that fits the motor trade description of 'previously owned'. Yacht brokers (never to be confused with second-hand car salesmen) are more straightforward and usually refer to such craft as, simply, 'used boats'.

Whatever you (and the broker) decide to call it, you are likely to consider a second-hand boat as your first sailing cruiser.

Why buy second-hand?

There are a number of reasons for buying second-hand, rather than new. The most important is likely to be money: the type of boat you have chosen costs less and may include a number of extras giving you more boat for the same amount of money. Even comparing two relatively modern cruisers, one brand new and one, say, three years old, the saving on the latter is likely to be significant (although, as we saw in Chapter 2, not as dramatic as with, say, a car). In addition, the older boat will likely have more gear included in the price.

Most but not all builders sell what is termed a 'basic' boat, giving the purchaser a variety of options as to what extras to have on board. Happily nowadays most basic safety equipment is no longer considered an optional extra, but even so the difference between the originally quoted price and the final invoiced figure can amount to a hefty, not to say startling, sum. With a two- or three-year-old boat, there are unlikely to be such surprises, and the quoted price is more likely to be the final price.

There is also the consideration that the previous owner will quite likely have put aboard more extra equipment than you could initially afford, from satellite navigator to weather fax, from Bimini top to bathing ladder. All this extra gear, which would be added to the invoice for the new boat, you will get for 'free' when buying a used boat. 'Free' is a relative term, you understand.

The classics live on

Some boats you will only be able to buy second-hand. We have already seen how boats in general hold their investment value, because of their relative longevity. This longevity extends not just to the structure, but also to the design. While a 20-year-old car will be significantly lacking in the features that come as standard on today's car, and these features will affect the performance and even safety of the vehicle as well as its comfort and convenience, the same is not so true of boats, at least of cruising boats.

Many of the boats that were in production 20 years ago and are no longer

The Westerly range – despite the various changes of ownership of the company – remain classics of British cruising design and deservedly popular as second-hand buys. Photo: David Harding.

in production now have become and are classics. From the van de Stadt Invicta to the She 36, and even the humble Westerly Centaur, you can only find such boats on the used boats market: they are (at time of writing) out of production and unlikely to be put back. Yet they remain very desirable, eminently enjoyable boats and, provided they are in good condition, will continue to be very good buys.

A little word of warning

Be careful, however, of so-called classics being put back into production by other than the original builder. There are some – such as the Contessa 32, being built again (2003) by Jeremy Rogers who first gave this timeless classic life – whose re-appearance can only be welcomed. However, there are others about which one might properly have more than a few misgivings. An essential question is 'why did the boat go out of production in the first place?' In some cases the answer might have been commercial misfortune befalling the builder, who was probably a better boat-builder than he was a businessman. In other cases it might have been that it was not a particularly good boat.

In the late 1970s and again in the 1980s, a number of boats went through a succession of builders, which, one after another, went bust – or at least ceased trading. A few months later, the boat would be back in production again. What was happening was that, as the builder ceased business, so the liquidator moved in. The two major assets of the failed business would be the premises, and the tooling – the moulds for the boat. The latter would be sold off by the liquidator to recoup at least some of the losses for the business's creditors (along with liquidator's fees). These were bought by some other entrepreneur at a fraction of the cost it would have taken to tool-up for a new design. The boat went into production again – only for that venture to fail too. While such a cycle did much for the liquidation trade, it did not do a lot for the hapless boat-buying public, whose interests would have been better served by someone taking a chain saw to the awful things and putting us all out of our misery.

A variation of this phenomenon occurred when some builders, although remaining in business, decided for sound commercial reasons to cease production of a particular model. Often, this would be because the boat, employing outdated construction techniques, would have become too expensive to build economically. Instead, however, of destroying the moulds one or two could not resist the temptation to realise what cash they could from them and sold them on, usually to a smaller firm. Too frequently, this new builder would lack what we might call the rigorous approach to quality control employed by the original firm, and apply economies. What the market ended up with was a much inferior version of what had once been a good boat,

trading on the reputation of the early versions. Happily, changing production methods and cultures (including fewer but larger suppliers of new boats) have substantially brought an end to this phenomenon which is now not nearly so prevalent.

So even when buying a 'classic', it would pay to make enquiries about which regime the boat was built under. If she was built by the original manufacturer, well and good. If, however, she was built by someone who acquired the moulds after the original builder ceased production, be wary and, if you can, call in a surveyor with specific experience of that particular model.

Lower down the scale

Further down the price scale, second-hand may well be your only option. Put at its baldest, you don't get much in the way of a new sailing cruiser these days for under £15,000 if not £30,000 but you can still buy a perfectly good second-hand sailing cruiser for that price. A glance in the window of any broker, or through the brokerage and classified columns of any of the magazines, will highlight the price differences between new and second-hand boats, and will illustrate the huge pool of used boats available on the market.

This is of course especially true of smaller cruisers – by smaller we mean under about 27ft (8–9m). (Incidentally, boats remain one of the last strongholds of Imperial measurement, sometimes iconoclastically so. Even countries where metric measurement has always been the standard and Imperial never known, will often refer to a boat of

(Opposite) *In the early 1980s, the 24ft Cornish Crabber was the first of a new breed of old-fashioned designs built with modern materials and methods. Still in production, her eponymous builders also now produce both the smaller Shrimper and the larger Trader.* Main photo: David Harding. Inset photo: Cornish Crabbers.

around 10 metres as a 'thirty-footer', while more than one sales brochure has stated that such-and-such a boat, loa shown as 8.2m, carries 250sq ft of sail.)

Once again, you will often get, included in the price of the boat, equipment that you would have to buy for a new boat: inflatable tender and paddles, knives, forks, spoons and plates, even binoculars, first aid kit, torches, fenders and boathooks.

Why buy new?

One very obvious reason is that you do not want a boat that someone else has owned: you want a new one. The new boat will almost always be in better condition than the used boat, and the gear and equipment will be at the beginning of its working life. The engine will have its full quota of hours to run, the running and standing rigging will not (or rather, should not) need to be renewed for several seasons. You might not be able to buy some boats second-hand, as they have not yet come on the market. This is likely to be the case with new designs in middle and larger size boats, especially those built on a semi-production rather than a full production basis (that is, the construction of the boat is not started until someone has ordered it).

A very good reason for buying new is that you will be dealing with a public entity – a company – which is required by law to act within the constraints of the myriad pieces of consumer legislation now on the statute books. If there is something not satisfactory about the boat when you finally take delivery,

it should be easier to have the matter rectified than if you have bought either through a broker or private seller. At least you will have a more easily identifiable target for your complaint, while if the company is a major force in the market it may be keener than an individual to protect its reputation, and so be more amenable to putting right what you perceive to be the problem.

By dealing with a company which sells boats all the time you may find it easier to get advice, or indeed to find the finance needed for the purchase, than if you are dealing only with a private individual. This observation applies, of course, equally well to dealing with a yacht broker in the purchase of a second-hand boat.

Probably the most important single advantage of buying new is that you will be buying a boat without a history, and all that that might entail. There should, next time the boat comes out of the water or indeed next time she is put in the water, be no nasty surprises.

There is another reason, no less real because of its intangibility. There is nothing quite like having our own boat 'built'. Even if, in the age of factory production, your boat is but a clone of many others coming out of the factory at so many a week or a month, your boat will probably have your name on it soon after the hull has come out of the moulds. If you possibly can, go and visit the factory or yard, and see your boat being built. As you drive there, you will be going to see it. As you drive back you will have seen her.

And after all, someone has to launch the boats for others to buy.

1

Brokers and Surveyors

Unless you are buying a new, or very small boat, your quest for your first sailing cruiser will eventually bring you into contact with one and probably both of these lubricators of the smooth machinery of exchanging yachts. Both are agents – and it is important to understand whose agents they are.

The broker, like the house estate agent, is primarily the agent of the seller, however there is a difference between the roles of yacht broker and estate agents. Whereas the estate agent is on only the side of the seller, the broker is properly more of a middle man. The broker will (one had more cautiously say should) see the transaction through from start to finish, acting as negotiator between the two parties, conveyancing the sale, holding the money (in a separate clients' account) until the sale is complete. Some brokers will undertake to find the particular craft or type of craft you are looking for, but this is still a fairly unusual arrangement, especially at the first-boat end of the market. The broker is most usually the seller's agent.

The surveyor, on the other hand, is usually the buyer's agent – although here, too, there is something of a caveat. It may well be you who appoints – and pays – the surveyor, but the surveyor himself (or herself) will cherish his objectivity. This will be partly a matter of professional pride – and partly because he does not want to be sued by a disgruntled vendor for having unjustifiably damned a good boat just so that you can haggle down the price. It is the surveyor's job to report to you in an impartial and objective manner the condition of the craft you have asked him to survey.

Choosing a broker

Brokers and brokerage firms, like estate agents, come in all shapes and sizes. There are independent brokers operating out of just one office, and there are large firms with offices in several locations. Many specialise in one particular field – some even in one particular make or manufacturer. Quite a few are linked to a manufacturer: one department of the firm acts as agent for new boat sales, another department of the same firm handles second-hand sales. This last will be concerned mostly with trade-ins – usually customers trading up, from a smaller to a larger. Such an office will normally have on its books mostly boats of the make in which it specialises, and just a few other odds-and-sods which the new boat sales department has taken in part-exchange. So if you have set your heart on a particular make – a Moody, a Hunter, a Beneteau, say – it pays to go straight to the company handling new sales of that make and talk to their brokerage department.

Other brokers will specialise in boats of a particular size or price range – naturally size and price tend to go together. Few brokers with boats varying from 45–60ft on their books will be able to offer you much for £10,000. Indeed, because the broker is a middle man and thus adding an extra layer to the price of the boat, few brokers at all will have much on their books for £10,000. Not much fat on that particular pig.

By the same token, brokers who do have smaller boats on their books tend not to have much in the way of larger craft.

How the broker operates

As a buyer, you need to know a little of how a broker works to help you judge the worth of what you are being told. Sellers of specialist boats will often put the boat for sale with just one broker – this is called sole brokerage. The majority, especially if they are keen to sell, place their boat on the books of several brokers, and invite them all to sell it. Since the broker works on commission – no sale, no fee – you might think that this element of competition would urge the brokers to greater effort in trying to sell the boat. Not necessarily so. Brokers will normally put most effort into selling their sole brokerage boats, since on those they are guaranteed a commission, so it is often those you will see most heavily pushed in the brokers' advertisements.

Bear in mind, also, that it will usually be the seller, not the broker, who is paying for the advertisement of the boat, especially if you see it in a magazine. The broker passes on to the client (ie the seller) the cost of the advert.

The broker will usually take about 8% of the final negotiated price as commission: the seller pays this. You, as buyer, should pay no commission to the broker, although you do normally make the cheque out to the broker, not to the seller. There are, however, some things you might immediately find yourself paying for – storage, for example, if the boat is stored in the broker's yard or berthed in his marina. If the boat is ashore and you want it delivered somewhere else, the cost of that delivery will be paid by you unless you have negotiated otherwise in the deal.

If you get this far with a broker, the relationship begins to change. No longer is the broker simply and solely the seller's agent – he may become your agent once he starts to make arrangements on your behalf. You need to be aware always of whom the broker is working for: the seller, or you. Dealing with a brokerage department of, say, a marina or boatyard, you may find yourself introduced to (handed over to, if you like) another individual from the yard who will discuss how you will take delivery. Or you may find that the salesman with whom you have dealt all along makes these arrangements for you – either way it is important at the outset to identify on whose behalf the arrangements are being made, what is in the purchase price, what is not and to know when the meter with your name on it starts to tick. Usually you will find that the joy of paying for a boat follows pretty swiftly after the initial joy of owning it.

With an independent broker, the distinction is likely to be more visible, especially if the boat herself is lying somewhere else. Again – you should be careful to tie up all the details of how you take delivery and who pays for what. It is especially important, before buying, to find out what bills if any remain owing, and to whom; you do not want to buy a boat then find that the yard or marina will not release it to you until you have settled the previous owner's outstanding accounts.

Much of this the broker may do for you. Part of the broker's job is to ensure that the vendor of the boat has proper title; this means there should be a complete history of the boat and all her owners from the day she was launched, with each sale properly recorded and verified. It also means that the broker should have checked that there is, for example, no outstanding mortgage or other charge on the boat. Some boatyards in their terms and conditions acquire a lien on boats placed with them; a lien is a legal term which gives the yard the right to hold on to (even sell) the boat if bills accrued on her have not been paid. It is the broker's job to ensure that all these matters are settled and clear before he offers the boat for sale. We

Many brokers base themselves in or near marinas, so you can often see several of their boats together, rather than merely poring over leaflets or driving miles to look at only one craft. Photo: Brixham Marina, MDL.

look at some of those aspects in more detail in Chapter 7.

A yacht broker is – or should be – more than merely someone who brings buyer and seller together. In effect the broker should be the holding agent for the boat and everything to do with her while the sale goes through. He (or she) sees the transaction through from beginning to end. In financial terms this means that the broker normally acts as stakeholder for both buyer and seller. Brokers who belong to one of the professional bodies – in Britain the best known is the AYBA (Association of Yacht Brokers and Agents) are required by their Association to keep separate client accounts for such money. This gives you a safeguard should the broker go bust when you are half-way through buying your first sailing cruiser through his office. You should certainly check with a broker

what will happen to, for instance, any deposit you pay to secure an option while the survey is being carried out. The RYA's strong advice is that both buyer and seller are safer when using an AYBA broker. Another set of initials you might see or hear is YBDSA – Yacht Brokers, Designers and Surveyors Association. This is the umbrella organisation for the AYBA.

Doing without a broker – magazines and marts

You will usually find your broker by looking in one of the yachting magazines, getting the brokers' addresses, writing to the ones who seem to have your sort of boat and asking for their list. Probably you will, at the same time, tell the broker what size or price range you are interested in, to save wasting time with unsuitable boats.

If, however, your requirements are modest, you may well be able to find your boat without going through a broker. Smaller – hence cheaper – boats are often sold by being advertised by their owners in the semi-display or classified sections of the yachting press, or with one of the specialist classified magazines.

Should you decide to be, in effect, your own broker it is you who must look out for many of the traps – title, unpaid VAT, clearance from the yard where the boat is lying – which you could normally expect the broker to take care of for you. While this book certainly does not set out either to replace the broker or turn the first-time buyer into a professional expert, it is the avoidance of many of those traps that are the subject of most of the other chapters.

Discussing the price

With or without a broker, you will almost certainly want to discuss the price of your putative purchase with the seller, rather than pay the straightforward asking price. There is, of course, an obvious vicious circle here: nobody expects to pay the full asking price, so nobody asks the price they realistically expect to get or indeed are prepared to accept. That this is silly is self-evident. It is also the way of the world. So the question becomes – how do you formulate your offer?

Some folks (I am one) advertise my boats, when I come to sell them, at the price I expect to get and tell callers that the price asked is the price expected and has been set with the boat's condition and known short-comings in mind. I do not always sell my boats at the first attempt.

Most people, however, build in a cushion. Sometimes the cushion is more of a wish than even a hope, and reflects the level of the owner's desire to sell the boat. There is an old broker's saying that all boats are always for sale – it's just that no one wants to pay the

price the owner currently requires to be parted from her.

Thereafter, the gap between asking price and acceptance price tends to diminish as the urgency of the need to sell increases. 'Realistically for sale' is an expression often used by sellers to convey the message that they are not joking, they really want to sell and the asking price has been fixed accordingly; 'seriously for sale' is like 'realistically for sale', only more so.

How often – and for how long – the boat is advertised is also a good indicator of how close to the real price the asking price has been set. Owners selling privately will often take a wishful punt at what they would like to get, but a broker will usually be quick to advise an owner who is expecting too much. If the owner persists, the broker is unlikely to waste too much time pushing a boat he knows he is unlikely to sell.

Certainly, it is always worth asking both the private seller and the broker if the price is negotiable and if you can make an offer.

Getting a survey

Even if only to help you negotiate the price you should have a survey made of anything other than the smallest boat – but the real reason for having the survey is so that you know what you are buying.

Indeed, there are a number of circumstances where you are effectively required to have a survey, the proper term is condition survey – of the boat. If you intend to take out a marine mortgage, the finance house will require a survey before issuing the mortgage. This is likely to apply to other forms of finance as well, such as bank loans. If the boat is more than ten years old it is highly likely that the insurance company will require a condition survey before

(Opposite) For the survey, the boat will have to be ashore to allow the surveyor to check the areas such as the keel, not accessible when she's afloat. Photo: David Harding.

insuring it for you; if the boat is built of wood the age may well be lower. The survey is to such institutions what the MoT certificate is to motoring law.

In any case, you would be very foolish to buy something as complex and expensive as a second-hand sailing cruiser without having a condition survey carried out by a qualified professional surveyor. Usually, the survey is such an integral part of the buying process that you will initially do the deal with your seller, or the broker, 'subject to survey'. This means that you agree to buy the boat unless the survey shows up something that reasonably allows you to have second thoughts. Very often there is a further round of negotiation over the price, with either the agreed price being reduced by all or a proportion of the costs of rectifying any defect found by the survey, or with the seller agreeing to put right any faults.

You could ask the broker, or the yard where the boat is lying, for information on local surveyors, but you should, however, instruct the surveyor yourself – and indeed the most reputable brokers may well decline to do any more for you than give you a list of local names. Certainly, the broker should not appoint the surveyor, for fairly obvious reasons not the least being that you want an unbiased opinion. However, since you will have to pay expenses, including travelling to the boat, it may pay to use a local surveyor, unless there is strong reason to chose someone else.

In order to carry out a complete survey, the surveyor will require the boat out of the water. This may already be the case, if not you or your broker will need to arrange for her to be slipped. The surveyor will also examine the boat 'as presented' which means that if there are areas of the boat not easily accessible – concealed behind linings for example, or even under screwed-down sole boards – the surveyor may not look there. You might think it a fairly hefty fee to pay to a chap who won't even unscrew a floorboard but that's the way it is. In

fairness, it must be said that the surveyor is there as your agent, not the agent of the vendor, and the boat is not yet yours, much less the surveyor's. So taking it to bits is not really part of his remit. On the other hand, the more of the boat you can arrange to have exposed, the better.

You will also need to establish with the surveyor beforehand whether or not the survey will include machinery, electrics and similar internal plumbing or whether he will look at only the condition of the main fabric of the boat: hull, keel deck, etc. Some surveyors require special instructions to look at these things. It is very difficult, for example, to survey an engine thoroughly without taking it apart which in the case of a boat's engine, usually involves removing it first. Primarily, the surveyor's job is to examine and report on the condition of the vessel's hull (which term includes decks, deckhouses and other parts of the fabric). The spars and sails also need to be made available to the surveyor if you wish to have a report on the condition of these.

The survey report

When you get it, you will almost certainly wonder why you bothered. The reason will be that the report will probably be couched in the vaguest and most non-committal of terms. Phrases such as 'appeared to be' and 'considering the age of the vessel' are likely to abound. Equally, the report may read as if it is the surveyor's considered opinion that no one in their right mind would buy – let alone sail – a vessel in a condition such as is this one.

This is because, first, the surveyor has to be very careful of what he says in an open report. Second, the surveyor has to be careful to restrict himself only to facts, or at least to observations which he can subsequently prove. At the same time, he must ensure that anything that might be a problem is brought to your attention in the report; the surveyor will be legally liable for the cost of rectifying any defects he has missed through negligence.

Do not be too dismayed if the report at first reading appears too shrouded in caveats and let-out phrases to be of much use for deciding whether or not to buy the boat. If there is compelling reason against buying, a well-written survey will lead the reader inescapably to that conclusion. Likewise, if the boat is a good buy the survey will almost certainly show it – even if you have to read it a couple of times to be sure. Discussing the report informally with the surveyor, preferably face to face rather than over the telephone, is a most excellent way of making sure you have spotted everything that has been written between the lines.

One thing to check when you select your surveyor is whether he has full professional indemnity insurance. The likelihood of a surveyor failing to detect a serious fault is in reality fairly limited, but mistakes can be made and unless the surveyor carries insurance you may find yourself without financial redress. Most surveyors are members of a professional body such as the Royal Institution of Naval Architects, the Institute of Marine Engineers or the Yacht Brokers, Designers and Surveyors Association (YBDSA). Membership of the Yacht Brokers, Designers and Surveyors Association is limited to those with relevant qualifications or experience, and the YBDSA insists on all its surveying members carrying full professional indemnity insurance.

Bad eggs

There are occasional bad eggs in this as in all businesses. Leaving aside the criminally intentioned – happily a very rare occurrence – the most likely problem area in brokerage is the one who is there merely to dabble, the chap who talks a good sale, but who does not actually achieve a lot (and in this, as in all else, one must always avoid confusing activity with achievement).

In the survey world, the greater difficulty probably lies in differing standards. Some surveyors are notoriously finicky, picking up on every little detail. While this may seem a good ploy when it comes to beating down the price, too much nit-picking may undermine the credibility of the argument as a whole. Others are notoriously non-committal, while a few surveyors seem to fill their report with a list of the things they were unable to examine, which may rather make you wonder why they bothered to go to the boat in the first place.

The main professional body for both brokers and surveyors is the YBDSA. They have both a process for vetting applicants, and a code of practice for those in the profession. Both professions – brokerage and surveying – are relatively small and it is one in which nearly everyone knows everyone else. While this can sometimes lead to cosy relationships, it also means that judicious enquiry on your part can often help you avoid some of the better-known accident black spots.

Should you feel that either the broker or the surveyor has failed you professionally, the YBDSA has an arbitration service which can sometimes be used to settle disputes without the expense of courts and lawsuits.

6

Buying New

There are, of course, still some fortunate people who are both wealthy and motivated enough to have their new sailing cruiser specially designed to their requirements and built completely from scratch. Such a boat is, however, rarely a first sailing cruiser. Almost certainly it will not be long before you have your own firm ideas of what your ideal cruiser, custom-built for you, would look like and be equipped with, but for the moment we shall assume that the new boat you buy is a production boat.

Once you have made your choice, be it at a boat show, after trial sails of perhaps two or three types of boat or simply in the sales office of the company concerned, the actual purchase process begins when the salesman produces a contract for you to sign.

If you live close to, or can visit, the builder's factory or main sales office, you will probably be dealing directly with the boat builder. If, on the other hand, you live far from the builder's main operation you may be dealing with an agent. If you are buying an overseas-built boat you will probably be dealing with a company wholly or majority-owned by the builder, but registered in the United Kingdom; this will be purely a sales company which has its own supply contract with the builder.

There is more to say about agents at the end of this chapter; we deal first with the overall principles of the contract you will be asked to sign, and assume you to be dealing direct with the builder.

The contract

In an ideal world of unbroken promises, solvent builders and prompt deliveries there would be no need for a written contract to define the rights and liabilities of the parties. There is however so much scope for disagreement, misunderstanding and faulty recollection of what was agreed between parties that a written contract generally is regarded as essential.

The terms of the contract offered to potential buyers vary enormously from one builder to another. Every agreement involves a degree of compromise, and it makes good sense to take a close look at the proposed terms before any commitment is made.

So far as the buyer is concerned, the ideal contract would provide a fixed date for delivery with no stage payments being required, title (ie legal ownership) in the boat passing immediately upon the order being placed, two-thirds of the price paid on delivery and a full season's sea trials and testing carried out before the final instalment is paid.

An ideal contract from the seller's point of view would provide for immediate payment of the full price, no fixed date for delivery, property in the yacht being retained until delivery, and no need for acceptance trials or testing.

In practice neither approach could be regarded as realistic but it is worth detailing some of the more important provisions that should be incorporated in every contract. The main concerns you should have are:

London's famous International Boat Show, the last at Earls Court before moving to Excel – shop window for the industry and a splendid place to gather ideas for your first sailing cruiser, or even buy her. Photo: David Harding.

- What are you buying (that is, is it the model you are looking at, or a variation; what gear, sails, equipment is included in the price and what is a so-called optional extra)?
- When will you get it, and what happens if there is a delay in delivery?
- When do you pay for it?
- What happens if the builder goes bust when the boat is half-built?
- What happens if, after delivery, you have a problem with it?

If you are at all concerned at some of the terms – you are, after all, making a very substantial financial commitment – you should take a rain check (and a copy of the contract) and ask your solicitor to look over it for you. The RYA provides an advisory service for its members who may have doubts about a contract of this nature that they are being asked to sign; this service is well worth the cost of becoming an RYA personal member alone.

The contract and your statutory rights

Some standard form contracts will contain words to the effect that *no other agreement, representation, promise, undertaking or understanding of any kind unless expressly confirmed in writing by the company shall add to, vary or waive any of these terms or conditions.* Normally this would not be objectionable because it does not invalidate your statutory rights. But this sort of clause should be deleted if you are buying the boat at least partly on the basis of promises by a salesman (for example about the yacht's performance). If you have, for example, been told that the boat will achieve a certain speed in a certain strength of wind, or complies with a river authority's or a foreign country's technical requirements, that should be put in writing together with a statement to the following effect:

'It is expressly agreed that these additional conditions represent a further agreement as required under Clause ... of our Standard terms and conditions and where inconsistent shall prevail notwithstanding those terms and conditions'.

Stage payments and passing of property (title)

If the boat you are buying is already built and in stock, you may be asked to pay only in two stages: the deposit-with-order and the balance-on-delivery payments which are common with any purchase that has to be got ready for you and the preparation of which is going to take more than a few hours. If the builder's order book is full, all existing boats have already been sold and there is a wait for delivery, you may well be asked to make other payments, usually at specific stages of build. This is most common with smaller companies, or those who build on a semi-custom basis. Whichever system is operated, it is important that you check what happens to the money you have paid over if there is a subsequent problem, and at what stage the boat ceases to be part of the builder's stock-in-trade and becomes your boat.

In recent years, several well-known companies in the yachting industry have gone into receivership, often with considerable debts, and some resulting in customers losing deposits and part payments with no legal remedy. Where a boatyard with a number of part-built yachts on the site calls in a receiver,

his first action in assessing the value of the stock and work in progress of the company will be to examine the contracts and decide where ownership of the yachts in question lies. Your contract should make it plain that the part-completed hull and deck, and the associated engine and microwave, are yours, and not the builder's. Hopefully your builder will not go bust but contracts should always provide for the worst-case situation, not the hopeful.

The British Marine Federation (BMF) is the overall trade federation for boatbuilders and suppliers in Britain, and the majority (although not all) builders in the United Kingdom are members. The Federation has a standard new boat contract which many of their members use. This has a clause which states that:

'The craft and/or all materials and equipment purchased or appropriated from time to time by the Builders specifically for its construction shall become the property of the purchaser upon the payment of the first instalment under this agreement ... the builders shall however have a lien upon the craft materials and equipment for all sums due....'

Therefore in the event of liquidation or receivership the purchaser of a part-built boat is to some extent protected against the possibility of the part-built yacht going into the receiver's general compensation fund. Of course if a deposit has only just been paid, and no work has yet started on the yacht, the deposit will be lost, so it is desirable to pay by way of deposit no more than the buyer could reasonably afford to lose (typically deposits or first stage payments should be no more than 5–10%). Some contracts ask for up to 100% before you obtain title; in those situations you could lose the lot. The RYA's advice would be not to enter into such an agreement.

In contrast to the BMF standard form agreement, some boatbuilders propose in their contracts that *'until the company has received full payment for the craft the property in the craft shall remain vested in the company'* or words to that effect. Where the purchase price is divided into a small (say 5%) initial payment and one single final payment of the balance on delivery, this is perhaps not objectionable. Where a larger payment is required, typically one third of the total price, you as the purchaser are then at considerable risk until the boat is completed and the final instalment paid.

If you find yourself confronted with such a contract you should insist either on the substitution of the BMF standard form, or the provision by the builder of a banker's guarantee that, in the event of the builder having a receiver or manager appointed, or a petition or resolution to wind up the company, or performing any act of bankruptcy or proposing an arrangement with his creditors, the full amount of all money paid under the contract should immediately be refunded to you. Or you should think of buying a different boat, for if the builder is unwilling to discuss either of these options you need to consider carefully, not just the fact that you are taking a considerable business risk in putting down a deposit and part payment without any protection, but also why the builder is being so intransigent and unreasonable.

If your builder agrees to amend such a passing of property clause, you must also insist – as part of the contract – that he inform his insurance underwriters of your interest, otherwise his builder's risks policy may be invalidated.

Building risks insurance

From the moment the title in the boat passes to you, so will the risk. Thus insurance of some form is required. Normally this will be offered as part of the builder's overall yard insurance, but you may wish to make your own alternative arrangements or at least check with the builders that their insurance cover is adequate.

Damages for late delivery

The BMF standard form of contract includes, as an optional extra, a provision that *'if due to the builder's failure without reasonable cause to proceed with reasonable dispatch, the craft is not completed by the date agreed .... the builders shall pay the purchaser £.... in respect of each week or part of a week until the craft is completed as agreed damages for loss of use of the craft'*. The figure to be inserted is for agreement between you and the builder; in agreeing it, a useful guide is to consider how much it would cost you to charter a similar boat during the period you are now waiting for your own.

Not entirely surprisingly this clause rarely appears in the standard terms offered by many builders even if they are members of the British Marine Federation, and you may experience some resistance if you ask for its inclusion. It may be possible to agree that the clause should only operate after a fixed number of weeks beyond the delivery date unless the delivery date is of great importance to you. And you may find the builder may wish to increase the price to allow for the potential risk to him of agreeing to this clause. If you are buying at, say, a Boat Show so-called discount or other special price, the builder might well want to revert to the list price – you will have to decide which is the more important to you, the price or getting the boat on time.

Arbitration clause

The BMF standard form agreement provides that *'all disputes arising out of, or in connection with, this agreement shall be submitted to a single arbitrator to be appointed, in default of agreement, by the President of the BMF and the Chairman of the Council of the Royal Yachting Association and the provisions of the Arbitration Acts shall apply'*.

Since litigation, even at County Court level, is a relatively costly and protracted process, the inclusion of an arbitration clause can be of great importance providing the purchaser with a quick, inexpensive and simple means of resolving disputes, particularly as to price and quality of work, with the builder.

If the standard contract offered by the builder excludes this clause, you should ask that the contract be amended to include it.

Buying through an agent

Although most British yacht builders deal direct with their customers, the situation often arises where prospective purchasers, especially those living at a great distance from the builder's yard, will be told after initial inquiry to conduct negotiations and all further business through a local agent. This is the practice often adopted, for example, by Scottish companies when selling to yachtsmen resident in the South East, and by Southern companies when selling yachts to Northern Ireland or Scotland.

On the face of it, this seems a perfectly sensible arrangement; the agent is the 'man-on-the-spot' who knows the local conditions and, furthermore, is able to sort out problems without delay. You will also be reassured that you are dealing with a locally known personality rather than a distant sales manager.

However, one or two incidents involving RYA members have highlighted a potential danger in purchasing a new yacht through an agent. In one case the yacht concerned was found to have a defective resin mix over part of the hull and in another case a fault in the hull/keel joint. When the owners sought the assistance of the agents from whom they had bought the yacht they found they had gone into liquidation. In one case the owner then asked the builder concerned to pay for the rectification of the fault, but was immediately reminded that there was no contractual relationship between them and thus (in the absence of negligence, which is always more difficult to prove than simple contractual liability) no liability arose.

If, therefore, you find yourself being asked by the builder to deal through an agent, you should think strongly of entering into a collateral agreement with the builders. This agreement would ensure that should the agent for any reason be unable or unwilling to perform his obligations under the express or implied terms of the main contract, then the builders will accept whatever liability would have attached to the agent. A simple exchange of letters between you and the builder to this effect will be sufficient to put the collateral agreement on a firm legal footing. A suitable draft for the builder to sign is given in Appendix 1 of this book.

Dealers and dealerships

The difference between a dealer and an agent is that the dealer buys the boats from the builder (albeit on some form of deferred payment scheme) before he sells them to the customers, while the agent holds little or no stock – perhaps a demo boat or two – and handles the sale as, literally, the builder's agent. It is a distinction that in the boat-buying market is often blurred; in the sailing cruiser world there is simply not the volume of business to support the sort of dealership franchises one sees in the motor trade. Nonetheless, it is important you establish which type of business – agent or dealer – you are dealing with. In the latter case, your contract will be with the dealer.

Normally, the rule of thumb is that if you can see and take delivery of the boat on the premises of the person or firm from whom you are buying, that person or firm is probably a dealership but if you are buying a boat that is not yet built, the person from whom you are buying is, if not the actual builder, then an agent.

(Opposite) *No matter whether you buy new or second-hand, you should have a sail either in the boat you are going to buy, or a boat of that class.* Photo: David Harding.

Acceptance trial

An acceptance trial is provided for as a matter of course for a one-off boat, but not always for a series-produced yacht. Nonetheless, unless the builder actually produces all its yachts off a production line to an identical specification, like a car manufacturer, it makes sense to retain part of the purchase price (typically 5% or 10%) until after you have had a reasonable opportunity to test the yacht in suitable conditions (ie not a flat calm). You should be given the opportunity to give the engine, gearbox and drive shaft a good run, and to make sure all the sails fit the spars (you would be surprised how often it can happen that, for example, the spar supplier changes some fitting without telling the builder or the sailmaker, and you then find that the headboard of the mainsail will not fit the luff groove, or the rings on the boom to take the reefing lines are not there). You need also to test all optional extra equipment both by itself and while other equipment is in use (beware, for example, the effect of an unshielded microwave oven or a high powered battery charging circuit on your GPS or autopilot).

The standard BMF agreement provides for the purchaser to be given 28 days' notice of the readiness of the craft for an acceptance trial on a stated date with the proviso that if the purchaser or his agent fails to appear for the trial, then after 7 days the trial will be deemed to have taken place and to have been satisfactory.

The acceptance trial normally takes place in waters convenient to the building yard, or in the case of an imported boat, to the yard or marina where the UK agent or subsidiary is based. This is only reasonable, since the builder may need to call upon his in-house resources to fix any minor problem shown up in the trials.

Of course, it is sometimes the case that an acceptance trial may not be possible, particularly in the case of a trailer-borne boat

which is being delivered over a distance to where you intend to keep it, or a boat that is to be delivered overseas. Nonetheless, if your putative builder or his salesman will make no provision for an acceptance trial (a single weekend will usually suffice) ask yourself why.

Since this is, by definition, your first sailing cruiser you may feel that you yourself have insufficient knowledge to conduct the acceptance trial. In that case, it might be worth engaging the services of a surveyor to come with you and go through the boat with the builder on your behalf. Naturally, you would want to go along too, if only to learn where all the switches are.

Statutory protection for boat buyers

The fact that an acceptance trial is satisfactory and that defects on your new boat do not come to light until later does not mean that you have no remedy. You have a number of statutory rights which cannot be affected by any provisions to the contrary in the contract.

A yacht, of whatever value, is a chattel within the meaning of the Sale of Goods Act 1979 and you will have all the protection afforded to private consumers by that Act. The most important sections from the yacht buyer's point of view are as follows:

Section 12
This imposes a condition that the seller has a right to sell the goods. If he is not the owner, or a third party has an interest in the goods, the condition implied by the Act will operate to protect the buyer whether or not the seller knew of his defective title.

Section 13
This imposes a condition that, where goods are sold by description, any inaccuracy amounting to a 'material mis-description' will give the right to repudiate the contract or to

For some people this handsome Moody will be the boat of their dreams. But the cost of this gleaming beauty will probably be the equivalent to the price of a holiday cottage in the West Country. Photo: Moody, Southampton.

claim damages. This section would be relevant to you where for example the agreed specification of a vessel was changed. Even if the seller is willing and able to carry out work to rectify the complaint, the consumer is still entitled to repudiate the agreement (unless the complaint is of a minimal or trivial nature).

Section 14

This repeats the old common law rule of *'caveat emptor'* (let the buyer beware) subject to provisos that goods sold in the course of a trade or business must be of satisfactory quality and fit for the purpose for which they are required. The section defines satisfactory quality as being as fit *'for the purposes ... for which goods of that kind are commonly bought as it is reasonable to expect having regard to any description applied to them, the price (if relevant) and all the other relevant circumstances'*. The seller is not held to guarantee that the goods are absolutely suitable, but even a minor defect making the goods unfit will give the buyer the chance to reject the goods so long as he does so in good time. For example some river authorities have particularly stringent construction and equipment standards. If, to the knowledge of the seller, the boat is being bought with those standards in mind and it fails to pass the scrutiny of the authority's inspector, the buyer is entitled to repudiate the contract unless the defect is really trivial. Alternatively, the buyer may either claim damages or accept an offer by the seller to remedy the defect.

In dealing with cases under the Sale of Goods Act, there are two important principles to remember:

* Do not delay in pursuing your rights; if you do not act immediately on discovering a defect, the court may decide that you have 'accepted' the fault, or you may be judged to have had enough use to prejudice your rights to full redress.
* Always pursue your complaint against the seller, not against the builder, supplier, sailmaker, engine manufacturer, sparmaker etc (unless they happen to be the same person). Do not be put off by the seller referring you back to the manufacturer; the seller is the only one under a direct obligation under the Sale of Goods Act to put matters right. You need only be concerned with additional guarantees provided by component makers if the seller of the goods himself is unable to satisfy his contractual obligations.

This does not mean, of course, that the seller may not arrange for the repair to be carried out by the person best qualified to do so,

particularly in the case of specialised equipment.

Misrepresentation Act 1967

This Act provides that any misrepresentation about the standard, quality or specification of goods, whether made innocently, negligently or fraudulently, entitles the buyer either to rescind the contract or to claim damages according to whether the misrepresentation was made innocently, negligently or fraudulently.

A seller must therefore be careful not to make unsustainable specific claims about a yacht's performance, whether as to engine performance, sailing ability or whatever. Even with new yachts there is great scope for misunderstandings between salesman and customer, and the buyer is always in a strong position if misleading statements have been made in front of witnesses.

Hopefully, of course, this book is the last you will hear, or need to hear, of all these important but potentially enjoyment-spoiling safeguards. The best contracts are those which are toughest to negotiate at the beginning of the deal and which never need to be referred to again. It pays at this stage, therefore, to be as meticulous, hard-nosed and unsentimental as you have ever been so that later, as you sit at her tiller with the wake hissing past your ear or lie in some quiet creek and enjoy the inexpressibly delicious smell of early-morning frying bacon, you can grow as sentimental as you like.

7

Buying Second-hand

Something like 80% of those buying a sailing cruiser for the first time buy what the motor-trade likes to call a 'previously owned' model. We sailors are not so fussy with our euphemisms and are happy to talk about buying a second-hand boat and, unless you are one of the 20%, this is what you will do. The RYA has produced a standard contract for use between two private individuals undertaking the sale and purchase of a sailing cruiser, and it is reproduced in Appendix 1. For the purposes of your intended purchase, we shall assume you will decide to use this contract, and that the seller agrees to this.

Parties to the sale

It may seem an obvious point, but one of the first things you need to do, once you have identified the boat you want to buy, is make sure you know exactly who is selling it. This is more than just the matter of checking title: you need to establish at the outset whether the boat is privately owned, or owned by the seller's company, and whether there is more than one owner. This latter might simply be the owner's wife, or it might be a sailing partner. Most sailing cruisers under, say, 30ft (9m) are owned in a straightforward way, as private possessions but even sailing cruisers as small as, say, 25ft (7.6m) are often owned by sailing partners. Once above 30 or maybe 35ft (9–10.6m), it is not uncommon to find that the person from whom you are buying the boat has some odd financial arrangement;

it might be owned by his business, or by some nominee company he has set up to fund the original capital. Such arrangements are quite common with boats where the original purchase price runs into six figures but we shall assume as a first-time cruising yacht owner, you will be looking for something a little more modest.

Even so, it is important to check that the person with whom you are about to deal is indeed the person who is actually selling the boat.

Discussing the price

We discussed brokers and surveyors briefly in Chapter 5. If the boat you are buying is over 35ft (10.6m) or the asking price well into five figures, it is most likely that the seller will have placed the boat with a broker, and you will be dealing with him. For the purposes of this chapter, therefore, we are thinking primarily in terms of a little cruiser, 27ft (8m) or under, which has been advertised in a magazine with an asking price of £12,000 ono (or near offer).

That 'ono' tells you at once he does not expect to get £12,000; indeed it is a positive invitation not to offer him £12,000 and to expect to pay less. Why people put such a foot-shooting phrase in advertisements is as much of a mystery as it is a tradition.

You telephone the number in the advert, and eventually speak to the person offering the boat for sale. He sends you some typed particulars of the boat, along with a couple of

Out of the water, you are able to see the condition of the hull – in the water, you will get the chance to try the boat under sail. Both boats are bilge-keelers which are ideal for drying moorings and shoal water cruising. The Duette (right), in particular, sails just as well as many a fin keel design of her size. Photos: (left) David Williams, (right) David Harding.

magazine write-ups that he has kept from around the time this particular model was new. You like what you see so far, and arrange to go and look at the boat.

Once you have seen her, you think you would like to buy her. Be rather careful what you do next. It is a common fallacy that a contract has to be written down to be valid. If he says 'I'm asking ten thousand for her' and you say 'that sounds fine – I'll buy her', the two of you have made a contract there and

then. If you have said it in front of witnesses, who are later prepared to remember the conversation in a court of law, you may well find yourself bound to buy the boat for that price no matter what is subsequently found to be wrong with her.

What you must say, if you have decided you want her and need to make sure she does not slip from your grasp, is 'I'd like to buy her, subject to survey', or better still '… subject to survey and contract'.

Paying a deposit

If you are buying the boat as a private sale, having seen her in an advertisement, for example, there should be no need to pay a deposit at this stage. If you are buying through a broker, the broker may ask for a deposit as an earnest of good faith on your part; also to justify his taking the boat off the market while you have the survey and other checks carried out. In particular a deposit may be requested if you are buying through a yard which will incur costs – for example slipping the boat – for your surveyor to do his job.

Depending on how badly you want this particular boat, you may agree at this stage to pay a deposit – although it is something you should avoid if you possibly can. Do they want to sell you the boat or not?

From your point of view, the smaller the deposit the better; after having read the survey you may decide you do not want to buy the boat. The buyer may then try to hold on to the deposit, claiming a variety of excuses: a lost selling opportunity, the cost of putting right any disturbance allegedly caused by your surveyor's examination. If push comes to shove you may have to enter into legal proceedings to get your money back – so the less you have at risk in the first place, the better. Ten per cent is a traditional deposit – but for no reason other than tradition.

As well as the deposit, you are about to spend more money before you buy, this time on the costs of the survey. These will include not just the surveyor's fee, but also any costs associated with having the boat hauled out for the survey. Having the boat ashore for the survey is pretty well essential. She may already be ashore, especially if you are buying during the winter, in which case you have saved a bit of money.

The survey

You really *must* get a proper survey done. The advice can hardly be repeated too often.

Surveyors belonging to the YBDSA usually charge a scale fee for a condition survey (see page 38) calculated on a simple formula which is roughly the length of the boat multiplied by the breadth and expressed in pounds sterling, so the scale fee for a boat 27ft x 8ft 6in (8 x 2.5m) will be around £230. Add in travelling expenses and you might still be paying less than £300. If your surveyor does not find enough for you to use to negotiate the price down by £300 the boat is clearly a very good buy and you should snap her up at the asking price. Surveyors and their reports are covered in more detail in Chapter 5.

You must decide at this stage, also, whether you want simply a hull condition survey, or whether you want to include all the gear that, supposedly, comes with the boat. Although it naturally costs more, including the gear and equipment in the survey is a good idea if only to establish a definitive list of what comes with the boat. The seller may have produced an inventory of sorts; the surveyor needs to be given a copy of this, as well as being given access to any store where the gear is kept if it is not already on the boat.

Engines are a problem. If the boat is ashore for the survey, as she should be, it may be difficult or impossible for the surveyor to run the engine and, in any case, many surveyors will specifically exclude the engine from their brief and suggest (or find for you) a specialist engineer. Most likely all that the surveyor's report will be able to do is confirm for you that the engine is there, and give a view as to its external appearance and condition. This is not quite as superficial as it sounds: if the engine is relatively new, in good visual condition and with no corrosion around its attached parts, it is probably in working order.

Once you have the survey report, the RYA contract gives you 14 days to decide on your next step. If the survey finds no material defects, then the contract obliges you to go ahead with the agreement but, as we have seen, such a report is less than likely and if it happens you know you are getting a good buy.

It is more likely that the survey will throw up something that causes you to ponder. You now have the option either of withdrawing from the sale and having your deposit refunded, or renegotiating the price to allow for the cost of making good the defects. Occasionally, the seller might offer to put right whatever is causing the problem at his own expense and within the original price. If that happens, you should insist that the repairs are carried out to your surveyor's satisfaction, and that the costs of his coming back to check the work is also met by the seller.

If you decide to pull out of the sale, you may find yourself in an argument about whether or not the defect which prompts your second thoughts is 'a material defect' within the meaning of the contract. There is no exact definition of what is meant by the term 'material', but a useful rule of thumb is if the cost of putting the problem right is more than 5% of the agreed price then that is definitely material, while if it is less than 1% the defect is not significant. Somewhere between the two will lie the dividing line, and it may well vary depending on the exact nature of whatever the surveyor has found.

Proceeding to completion

So you have decided to buy the boat, and agreed with the seller the final price. There are still quite a few things to check, however, before you part with your money:

- The seller's title to the boat;
- Once you have bought the boat, you haven't also bought a load of outstanding bills;
- There are no outstanding mortgages registered against the boat;
- VAT has been paid on the boat, and you can prove it.

You also now need to think about *where* you will buy the boat. This may sound odd. The boat is sitting in a boatyard, the man wants to sell it, you want to buy it – surely you buy it where it is sitting? Not necessarily so. You may not wish to become involved with that yard. It may suit you to take delivery of the boat somewhere entirely different. We shall look in more detail at this in Chapter 11; for the moment we need merely to bear it in mind.

Checking title

The vast majority of second-hand boat sales in the United Kingdom are conducted honestly between two people, neither of whom intends to defraud the other. A tiny minority involve some sort of intentional fraud of a serious nature, and a somewhat larger minority involve some sort of dispute between buyer and seller which may be as minor as the number of fenders left on board or may be rather larger.

Probably the most common cause of trouble, after actual defects in the boat, is the buyer discovering during or, worse, after the sale that some third party is now chasing him for money owed by the previous owner. The legal formalities surrounding the ownership of small sailing cruisers can be likened to the legal formalities surrounding the ownership of a bicycle or a toy train set. But the money involved is often closer to that of a house or at least a rather smart car. You as the buyer need to be particularly careful that what you are buying comes unencumbered with other people's claims. Caveat emptor – buyer beware – is still the rule, and although what follows may lead you to think the world of small sailing cruisers is peopled only by crooks, thieves and dubious practitioners, we are in fact mostly very nice people. And you should still check everything twice because now is the only time you will be able to walk away from the problem, if problem there be.

The starting point for checking the seller's right to sell the boat to you is the previous

Bill of Sale. The seller should be able to produce this for you, and let you have a copy. From it you should be able to establish whether, for example, the seller himself bought the boat in person, or through a company; and whether the seller bought the boat alone or in partnership with others.

Of course, the previous Bill of Sale will tell you only what happened at the time of the previous sale, not what may have happened since.

Checking the register

Checking the registers (see Chapter 10) is the next obvious step to be taken.

For a boat on the Part I Register, the name and Port of Choice (or initials of the owner's club) should be marked on the stern, and the official number either carved in the main beam or displayed on a plaque on the main bulkhead. The seller should also be able to show a certificate naming him as the registered owner. You can verify the details (including the engine serial number) with the Registrar in Cardiff (the address is in Appendix 7) and request a transcript of the registration particulars. This transcript should duplicate the information on the registration certificate, and in addition will also disclose whether any mortgage has been placed on the boat.

Even this, however, is not entirely fool-proof. The Register does not record any other transactions in connection with the boat while for boats on the Part III – formerly known as the Small Ships Register – there is even less guarantee since the information on the SSR is simply an unverified duplicate of the information originally supplied by whomever registered the boat in the first place. Even so, it is worth carrying out the check.

Other checks

Ideally, the seller should be able to produce for you documents of title showing the chain of ownership from the time the boat was built, through to the present time. These should include the original Builder's Certificate, the original receipted VAT invoice from the builder, and subsequent signed forms of contract and Bills of Sale from the first owner to the second, and so on.

The seller should also be able to produce a file of recent receipts in his name for mooring charges, harbour dues, insurance premiums, and maintenance and repair work and you should not be embarrassed to ask for these. In addition to assuring you of the seller's right to sell you the boat, they will also help to give you a picture of the way the boat has been kept and maintained in the past, and this will help you establish a fuller history of what you are about to call your own. If these receipts and bills are consistent and go back three or more years, then it is reasonable to assume that the yacht is his to sell.

Not every seller keeps a detailed file about the boat, especially if she is a small boat, but even if there is not so much as a previous Bill of Sale, the seller should still be able to refer you to someone: a yacht club secretary, a Harbour Master, a river or canal authority, or the boatyard who will be prepared to vouch for both him and the boat. If the seller cannot even offer this, then one can only repeat what the Romans learned the hard way: *caveat emptor*.

Unregistered mortgages

Checking on the absence of an unregistered mortgage is a rather more difficult matter. In the High Court case of The Shizelle (1992), it was held that an unregistered mortgage on an unregistered yacht was valid not only against the original borrower, but also against any subsequent owner whether or not he knew of the mortgage. Given that a number of leading finance houses lend considerable sums of money on the basis of unregistered mortgages, this creates an obvious danger for buyers. In recent years, an increasing number of cases

Survey tips

When looking at a boat that you are interested in buying, it is easy to do a preliminary survey at the same time. This will give you a reasonable idea of the boat's condition. If you like the look of it and feel it has potential then instruct a qualified surveyor to do a condition survey. Before doing any checking or before going on board make sure the boat is safe. If she is ashore, there should be tight, strong supports on both sides – about every 1.5m (5ft). Permission to look over the boat should be obtained from the owner or broker.

You will need a powerful flashlight; better still, a wandering lead plugged into the mains. This is a boon when looking into dark corners and even outside the hull.

The hull, deck and cabin top should have a smooth curvaceous shape, with no local unevenness, inwards or outwards. If the bottom has

patches of blisters, this probably means the boat has osmosis. The cost of curing this has to be taken into account, but the boat might still be worth buying.

Cracks in a hull are not always easy to detect. Try viewing from near the bow and stern, and looking obliquely along the topsides. This view will also show if the bulkheads are pushing the hull outwards slightly.

It is common to find a crack line between the top of a fin keel and the hull. This does not condemn the boat, but it will almost certainly need work, and this is the sort of thing to draw to the attention of the professional surveyor if you decide to make an offer for the yacht.

There should be no indentation inwards of the fibreglass hull at the fore or aft ends of the top of the fin. Inside the hull the structure which strengthens the hull around the ballast must be free from cracks and peeling glass.

The deck fittings often give a useful indication of the way the owner has looked after his craft. Cracked or broken stanchions, pulpits and handrails (usually easy enough to repair) suggest that the boat has not had much tender loving care.

The chain-plates (fittings bolted to the structure to which shrouds or backstays are attached) should show no signs of movement,

It is important to lift up the sole boards and look in the bilge. The aft end of the bilge in a wooden boat is a place to expect trouble.

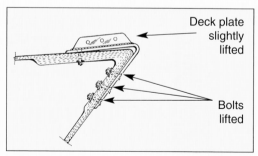

Deck plate slightly lifted

Bolts lifted

A glance over the bow may show that the bolts holding the stemhead fitting are tilted slightly. Then peer closely at the flat plate on the deck, and see if it has pulled up just slightly. This means there will be leaks through the deck, and in time the whole fitting may come adrift. Also, check the backstay chain plate for tilted bolts.

and the surrounding structure should not have any cracks, bumps, splits or other signs of failure. As the loads on chain-plates are very high, they need plenty of reinforcing all round. If a chain-plate is fitted to the side-deck and the adjacent coaming has a big window in it, there may be a weakness which can show up as leaks, cracks or distortion.

Have a good search right round the periphery of each bulkhead to see if the glassing onto the hull has peeled off or cracked. The same applies to the bonding of the mast support pillar and the furniture.

Items like sails, deck gear, cushions and even spars have to be replaced from time to time, so major defects here should not necessarily put you off buying the boat. But the price has to take into account the full cost of buying and fitting the new parts. The same applies to other general damage or signs of wear; most things can be repaired but the cost must be reflected in the price. Your professional surveyor will advise you. Often the owner and buyer have different ideas about replacement costs, so a firm quote from a boatyard or supplier is needed to settle the argument.

A rudder should move easily from side to side, when the tiller or steering wheel is put hard over both ways. However there should be no movement at the pintles or bearings. Rudder blades made of fibreglass quite often split down the front, along the bottom, or down the aft edge, and this can be serious, even if the fissure is tiny.

Without taking an engine apart it is impossible to find out its true condition. If the engine looks clean, well painted, and 'loved' then there is a fair chance that it will run well, at least for a season or two, provided it gets proper attention. If it looks tired, with rust in many places and signs of corrosion as well as water weeps and grubby black dribbles of oil, then the betting is that this engine is going to give trouble soon.

As a very crude guide, modern boat diesel engines will last about 20 years provided they are given care and maintenance. So if the boat is 16 years old, and the engine is the original one, it makes sense to start planning for a new engine in say two years' time.

Metal tanks should be well secured in place, so that when pushed or pulled they do not shift. Flexible tanks need straps or lashings to hold them in place, and they should not be lying on rough or sharp fibreglass or other structure.

The P-bracket which supports the propeller shaft outside the hull should not shift when pushed sideways. (Check that the hull is well supported before doing this.) If there are signs of cracks where the P-bracket goes into the hull, repair work is needed.

The propeller should be tight on the shaft, and not have any obvious damage like cracks, bent blades or chunks out of the blades. The shaft should not make clunking sounds when pushed sideways or upwards.

All the spars, including the roller-furling gear, should be checked for corrosion and cracks. These are most likely to be found near fittings. If the mast goes through the cabin top, shine a torch up from below in the cabin to see if there is corrosion or worse at this location. It is best not to take off the mast coat at this point as it may get torn, and the owner may demand a new one if the sale of the boat does not go through. Get the professional surveyor to arrange for the mast coat to be removed.

If possible, spread all the sails out on a spacious clean floor or dry, mud-free lawn. Look them all over for tears, worn stitching, unglued joins and signs of wear. In practice, this spreading out is seldom possible, so each sail is checked by pulling the corners out of the bag and looking at them for signs of trouble.

This feature has given you a few tips on what to watch out for when you first look over a potential purchase, but for more detailed surveying advice, see page ii for titles which deal with surveying small craft.

Ian Nicolson C. ENG. FRINA

have occurred where a buyer in good faith has had his boat repossessed by the defaulting seller's finance house. In some cases this does not occur until months or even years after the sale, and is usually triggered off by the seller missing one or more of his repayment instalments.

The only feasible means of searching out an unregistered mortgage is either to check with the boat's insurers whether there is another interest noted on the policy or in their files, or check with the leading finance houses whether they have an unregistered mortgage in respect of the boat.

Another check you can make is with Boatmark (see Chapter 10). This scheme, introduced in 1995 by the British Marine Federation, is intended to act as a financial register for all mortgages, loans and bank loans made against boats. If it worked the way the motor trade equivalent works it would be superb; (in 2003) Boatmark still has only 10,000 craft registered. For their own (no doubt very good) reasons, the major finance houses and banks have been slow to co-operate with the BMF and the scheme.

By definition, any scheme which relies on merely voluntary registration of loans and mortgages is bound to provide an incomplete register but, as with the rest of the advice in this chapter, the more information about the boat you can cross-check, the less likely you are to receive a nasty shock after you have bought it.

Liens

A lien is a legal concept which allows what would otherwise be an unsecured creditor to take an interest in a piece of property (in this case, the boat you are thinking of buying) as security against the unpaid debt. The bad news for you is that a lien can be taken out against a boat and, even if the boat is sold, remain in force. Worse, the fact that the new buyer was unaware of the lien's existence does not invalidate it.

Thus, although an entry for the boat you want to buy on the Part I Register indicates good title, and although any unregistered mortgages on a boat on the Part I Register are invalid against a bona fide purchaser who has been given no notice of them, it is still possible for some other individual or company to have a stake in the boat that you are trying to buy. To start with, the rule about unregistered mortgages applies only to boats on the Part I Register – if the boat is unregistered, or even on the SSR, an unregistered mortgage remains valid even when the boat is sold and even if the new owner is not told of the mortgage.

In addition, harbour authorities, marinas, boat repair yards, crew, salvors (if the yacht has been the subject of a salvage claim), victuallers, suppliers of equipment, or more or less any others you can think of, may all have a claim against the person selling you the boat, in which case they may also be able to claim a lien against the boat herself. This also extends to Customs and Excise if VAT has not been paid on the boat (or if the owner cannot prove that there is no VAT liability). It is, of course, quite impossible for you to be completely sure that there are no liens outstanding on the boat. The best you can do is ensure that the contract is signed (Clause 7.3, Appendix 2 deals with liens, mortgages etc) and ask at the marina office, the Harbour Master's Office, the yacht club or any other local contacts you can make if there are any known problems with the boat. Word of any unpaid bills, marina charges, harbour dues or salvage claims tends to circulate very fast, and the local grapevine is probably the best means of accessing this information.

(Opposite) *Many cruiser owners cannot resist the urge to do a bit of racing as well. Properly looked after, your first sailing cruiser will last for many years and be a sound investment in more than merely financial terms.*
Photo: David Harding.

At last – you buy the boat

Once you have completed all your investigations, agreed the price and worked out what you are going to do with her once she is yours, you can go ahead and buy the boat.

You should not hand over the final balance of the purchase price unless you are given all the documentary proof that will show that you are now the rightful owner. This will include a Bill of Sale made out by the seller and showing you as the buyer – it need not be a cumbersome document, and an entirely satisfactory template for such a document has already been drawn up by the RYA's legal work department and is given in Appendix 4.

The documentation should also include the boat's registration certificate, to enable you to re-register it in your name. If, for whatever reason, the seller is unable at the last minute to produce exactly the right documentation, you should insist on retaining at least part of the remainder of the price.

Now what?

At last, you have bought your first sailing cruiser. Congratulations. Now what are you going to do with it? Of course, you will already have made quite a few of those decisions: Insurance we look at in Chapter 9, and in Chapter 11 we look at Taking Delivery.

8

VAT

Value Added Tax (VAT) was introduced in the United Kingdom on 1 April 1973. Since then, any boat built in or imported into this country for private use since that date should have had VAT paid on it. Assuming:

- You are not a VAT-registered person or trader;
- You are buying the boat from another private individual who is not VAT registered;
- The boat itself has VAT-paid status;

then the resale of the boat from him to you does not attract more VAT. This applies even if you are buying the boat through a broker who may be VAT registered (the broker will charge the seller VAT on the commission – but that is not your problem). However, if you are buying the boat from, say, the brokerage office of a builder who has taken it in part-exchange and is now selling it on, VAT may well apply; so you need to establish that the price you are discussing is inclusive of VAT. As a matter of interest, it is now against the law in the UK for prices of VATable goods to be quoted ex-VAT when being offered for private sale. However, this regulation is sometimes flouted by boat sellers on the pretext that boats are not always bought by private individuals, but may also be bought by VAT-registered companies or by non-UK residents, both of whom are in a position to claim back the VAT from HM Customs & Excise. This ruse is particularly prevalent at boat shows, the worst offenders being those who are acting as agents for overseas builders.

Although VAT is not involved in a private sale within the United Kingdom and on a boat built in the United Kingdom, the question of not merely whether VAT has been paid on your boat (and whether you are able to prove it) is becoming increasingly important as the European Union moves steadily towards being one homogenous community for taxes and customs duty. Especially if you take the boat abroad, you may be required, and must be able, to produce documentary evidence either that VAT has been paid on the boat, or that it is deemed to have been paid – because, for example, the boat was either built in the UK before 1972, or was imported to the UK before that date and has been in private use ever since.

This means that when you come to buy your first sailing cruiser, the seller should provide you with the original VAT receipt for the boat, if she was new after 1972, or if she was imported, evidence that VAT was paid at importation. If she was built (or more correctly, first used in the UK) before 1972 you need the original and dated sales invoice or a builder's certificate showing when she was first supplied within the EU.

Unless the seller is able to produce proof that VAT on the yacht has been paid at some time, either in the United Kingdom or elsewhere in the EU, or that she is older than the introduction of VAT, you may find yourself facing, at some time in the future, a potential VAT assessment on the current value of the boat if at any time an EU customs official carries out a spot check. The existence of this threat is another good reason to put the boat on at the very least the SSR; customs officers tend not to start making enquiries on a properly registered British ship. In the absence of all else, at least carry with you the Bill of Sale showing that the yacht was bought by you, a UK resident, from another UK resident and therefore whether or not VAT has been paid is a matter for British customs jurisdiction.

Until the end of 1992 it was possible for a yacht built in the UK, for a UK resident, to be exported immediately upon completion without payment of VAT, for use overseas on a tax-free basis. The International Convention on Temporary Importation provided that all convention countries should permit the free use of recreational equipment and means of transport for tourist purposes for a minimum of six months in any one year. This rule was interpreted more liberally than the minimum in most European countries including France, Spain and Italy, and over the years tens of thousands of yachts built for northern European owners enjoyed tax-free status in Mediterranean marinas.

1 January 1993 saw the end of concessions of this sort between EU States. Apart from a few months' grace for yachts already enjoying tax-free status, any yacht in any EU State, owned by a national of any EU State for his private use, must be VAT-paid. In theory it should make little difference which state the VAT is paid in, since rates are intended to be roughly equivalent; in practice, however, some states tend to be considerably more flexible in agreeing modest valuations with owners, and allowing payments to be spread over an extended period. 1 January 1993 also saw the introduction of an amnesty for any yacht in the EC area built on or before 31 December 1995. Therefore, unless you are

able to prove either that the boat is VAT-paid or that she was built before 31 December 1995 and was in European Union waters on 31 December 1992 to 1 January 1993, you are liable to pay VAT on the current value.

VAT regulations are complex, and subject to such apparently frequent change and fresh interpretation that it seems that anything other than the most vague generalisations written about them is out-of-date as soon as it is published. If the VAT-paid status of your first sailing cruiser is not immediately and simply apparent from the documentation which the seller can show you, and hand over, then you need expert advice on the specific case of the boat you are thinking of buying. You can get advice on the current documentary evidence required to prove VAT-paid status, if you are an RYA member, from the RYA Sail Cruising Department at RYA House in Hamble, Hants.

In 1998, HM Customs and Excise produced a two-page fact sheet especially intended for UK cruising sailors who had concerns about VAT. It is published with this book as Appendix 5.

HM Customs used to have a special yacht unit based in Dover, where expert advice was but a 'phone call away' but this has now (2003) been disbanded and yacht VAT enquiries are, like all others, now handled by a so-called Helpline. This, after taking you through a lengthy recorded menu of irrelevant numbers and messages will eventually deliver you to a human. This invariably courteous individual may or may not know something about yachts and their VAT treatment, but for the answer to any complicated question you will probably be advised to write to your local 'written enquiries office', whose experts are supposed to give you an answer within 15 working days. Such is progress. Good luck.

9

Insurance

As soon as you take over title to your new boat, you take on the responsibility for it. Unlike owing and using a motor car, there is no law that requires you to insure your boat but there is so much scope for damage to the yacht, the crew, other people or other vessels in the ordinary course of owning a boat, never mind taking it to sea, that it would be foolish not to have comprehensive insurance cover. And having said there is no law requiring it, you will almost certainly find that many harbour authorities, marinas and boatyards will require you to have, at the very least, third party cover, possibly up to £1 million or even £3 million sterling.

Curiously, and again unlike motor car insurance, you will find there is very little difference in the premiums for third party cover only and fully comprehensive. The reason is simply actuarial: on the one hand the market is hardly big enough to warrant a two-tier structure, and on the other hand the real risk is that you are just as likely, in any accident, to damage another boat (or person) as you are yourself. This should be quite comforting, really; it shows us that boating (and in particular cruising under sail) is considered by those in the risk business to be a very safe pastime.

The insurance contract

Unlike the relatively simple policies used in household and motor car insurance, the standard yacht insurance policy is a complex document. It is difficult for the layman to

understand the contract fully without access to the Marine Insurance Act 1906 and the body of marine insurance case law contained in the Lloyd's law reports.

The yacht insurance market is highly competitive, divided between one group of specialist underwriters working at Lloyd's (who may be approached either through an agency or via Lloyd's brokers) and insurance companies (who may be approached either through Lloyd's or non-Lloyd's brokers or direct). In the insurance market as anywhere else you get what you pay for, and while it is wise to shop around you should not be tempted to go for the cheapest. It can often be the case that companies who work away from the cheaper end of the market will be more flexible in interpreting the strict terms of the policy in the case of difficult claims, and speedier in settling the more straightforward ones. It is also the case that one reason for a company being able to offer lower-than-the-average insurance premium rates is that the policy excludes most of the things you are likely to want to claim for.

When the 1995 European Directive on standard form contracts came into effect, most UK insurers introduced new policy wordings to comply with the rule that contract wordings should be readily understandable by the layman. While this is to be generally welcomed, as the old Institute Yacht Clauses were difficult to interpret, the new approach has given rise to a wide variety of policy conditions, and while one insurer's cover may seem very much less expensive than another's, it may be that a close and expert comparison of the policy document will show, as mentioned above, the cheaper company to be offering very much more limited cover. Although it may be going too far to say that the insurance market in general has used the requirement to re-write their policies into plain English as an excuse to narrow down the scope of cover intentionally, it seems quite clear that this is the practical result of the new wordings in a number of cases. The RYA legal affairs department's advice is that before agreeing to insure your sailing cruiser under one of the new policies, it would be wise to ask the broker or underwriter to confirm in writing that the new policy will provide at least the same cover as that provided by the 1985 Institute Yacht Clauses.

Premiums and insured value

Yacht insurance premiums tend to run out at somewhere between 0.6 and 2.5 per cent of the declared value of the craft – low risk craft such as sailing cruisers are usually nearer the lower end of the range. If you are quoted a higher rate, it is worth asking why and seeking to negotiate as the nature of risk varies according to a number of factors:

- Is the mooring secure against extremes of weather?
- Is the area patrolled by police or harbour officials to discourage vandalism and theft?
- What is the intended cruising range?
- Does the owner have any significant qualifications?
- Has the craft been built to current BW (British Waterways) or NRA (National Rivers Authority) standards (and does the insurer regard that as relevant)?

Unless, however, you already know quite a lot about both boats and insurance, you may well find the broker or insurance company is

familiar with both the type of boat you are buying and the place you intend to keep it, and has set the premium rate accordingly.

One way to reduce the premium is to accept a larger-than-standard excess: the 'excess' is the amount you are prepared to pay yourself before the insurance company's liability kicks in. Somewhere between £200 and £300 excess is now fairly standard, but increasing it to, say, £500 could significantly reduce your premium. A word of caution, however: do not forget that the excess always applies; it is not a case of you pay if the claim is under £500, the insurance pays if it is over. You always pay the first £500, no matter what the total of the claim.

Another way to reduce your insurance premium is to join the RYA, and go on to gain RYA Yachtmaster qualifications. Many insurance companies offer discounts both to RYA members and, more importantly, to those who hold RYA competence qualifications.

Is a survey essential?

Most underwriters will be happy to insure a yacht up to 10 years old, without a survey being required, but if the boat is older than this, a survey is usually required. Usually, the survey is required only once, when you first put the boat on that insurer's books, but if the boat is wood-built and more than ten years old, a survey may be required more frequently.

Completing the proposal form

It is essential when completing the proposal form to put in the fullest and most accurate information and to answer all the questions literally. This is not a test to see how little information you can get away with giving – rather, think of it as a test the insurance company might apply in the event of a claim to see if they can get away without paying. This advice may sound a little jaundiced – but it is given for good reason. The proposal form constitutes the basis of a binding contract,

For most insurance policies to remain valid, you must ensure that when your boat is left unattended she is properly secured and locked up. Items such as outboards and inflatables should be either stowed away or fixed to the boat in such a way that they cannot easily be removed. Photo: David Williams.

and in the event of an insurance claim, most underwriters will re-examine the proposal to ensure that the claim is valid within its terms of reference.

The law recognises that insurance contracts are one-sided; the boatowner knows everything about himself, his boat and the nature of his proposed use of the boat. Since the insurer only knows what the owner chooses to tell him, he is protected by the legal principle of uberrima fides. Roughly translated this means that the insured must show the 'utmost good faith' in providing information and failure on your part to have done so when you filled out the proposal form could well entitle the insurer to refuse to pay the claim on the grounds that your contract with him is not valid. It is, of course, in the very nature of things that such a problem becomes evident only when you make your claim; by which time it is, of course, too late. Bear in mind also that the

insurance company can do this even if the information you omitted to give is entirely irrelevant to the subject matter or circumstances of the claim. It would also be wrong to think that this sort of thing happens only at the cheaper end of the market, where one might expect companies with dramatically low premiums to be correspondingly parsimonious when the time comes to pay up.

Cruising areas, laid-up periods and other matters

So far as the average UK-based boatowner is concerned, there are three main cruising ranges available at standard prices which must be declared on a proposal form. These are:

- Non-tidal waters within the UK;
- Coastal cruising within an agreed range of

the yacht's home port or permanent mooring;

- Full coastal and sea-going cruising within the 'home trade' limits, which cover all UK waters and continental coasts from Brest to Elbe (some policies may include continental inland waters as far south as Paris, but an additional premium is usually payable).

You need, too, to be careful if you intend to cruise to Ireland (and indeed, you should so intend some day – you will find the most wonderful cruising grounds opening up before you) as some policies do not include Ireland within the home trade limits definition.

The period in use and the period laid-up are also examined in the proposal form. The insurers are looking at two different things here: when the boat will be in use, and when not, and where she will be when she is not in use. Clearly, insurers will assess the risk to be higher if you intend to use the boat for twelve months in twelve as opposed to six months in twelve, less obviously they may also consider the risk to be higher if you use the boat in winter, when bad weather is more likely (albeit the risk of collision in crowded anchorages might be less). 'Laid-up' means in this context 'not in use' rather than specifically 'hauled ashore and set up on shores or in a cradle and with a cover over it', although there are also different risks involved with the boat afloat and the boat ashore. Many marina-kept boats stay in the water all year round, but are nonetheless laid-up by 31 October and put back in commission after 31 March. You must make it clear on the proposal form what your plans are.

Of course, your plans may change. Having opted for UK coastal waters you may decide, after all, to visit France or Holland, or the very lovely cruising grounds of southern and western Ireland. A late Indian summer may beckon you to sea into November, or you may suddenly decide on a short, crisp Christmas sail. None of these things represents a problem – but you must tell your insurers before you implement your changes of plan. Very often, the policy is altered and there is either no extra premium, or the cost is nominal.

Possibly, because they are thinking in terms of RIBs, small motorboats and other eminently stealable (and quickly saleable) types of craft, some policies and proposal forms have quite stringent restrictions concerning trailable boats. They will usually insist that if a trailed boat is not kept at home, it must be made secure in a locked compound, and if left afloat unattended, must at all times be on a secure mooring. This is fairly reasonable, but some policies insist that such a boat, when left unattended, be locked to the berth or mooring. This is almost impossible to adhere to on literally every occasion you have to leave the boat alone for a moment even with something like a RIB or speedboat: it seems unnecessarily Draconian in the case of a Hunter Medina, or Cornish Shrimper.

You will also need to be completely open about any intention to use the boat for charter, whether bareboat or skippered, or for any commercial purpose, including business entertaining. While these are not problems in themselves, underwriters will normally lay down conditions about the qualifications and experience of prospective charterers, and your premium may be loaded because of a perceived increase in your third party risk. Of course, once you get into charter work, a whole new ball game of regulatory compliance will open up for you, including the recently introduced (1996) DoT Code of Practice.

Opposite: What it's really all about. VAT and insurance, bank loans, surveys and legal agreements – as you wade through all those forms, keep in your mind's eye whither they will lead you. Just you, your boat, the sea and the sky …
Photo: David Harding

Insured value

Unlike motor insurance, where the value of a car in the event of a write-off is taken to be its current market value, marine insurance is based on the principle of agreed value. If a yacht is insured for, say, £10,000, and in the case of total loss the insurers are able to show that it would have fetched no more than £8,000 on the open market, they are still liable to pay the full figure. Provided you have not deliberately over-stated the value, there should be no argument on the matter. This does not, of course, exempt you from accurately stating the price paid on the proposal form; this is not necessarily the same as the value of the boat, but if there is a marked difference your insurers may wish to know the reason. If your boat is stolen rather than written-off by being, say, blown ashore from its mooring, you will probably be visited by some sort of investigative agent employed by the insurance company. Although ostensibly engaged to investigate the circumstances of the theft and, if possible, assist the insurers recover your boat for you, you will quickly realise that part of his brief is (even if the insurers try to deny it) to check up on you, and the claim you are making. Speaking from experience, this can be an eye-opening, not to say indignation-inducing, experience.

Just as bad as over-stating the value is under-stating the value, perhaps with the intention of reducing the annual premium, which is normally calculated as a percentage of the total insured value. Such a practice is likely to back-fire in the event of any claim, not merely total loss, because of a practice called 'averaging'. Basically, what averaging does is allow the insurer to pay out on a claim only a percentage equivalent to the relationship between the insured value and the actual value. So if your boat is worth, say, £16,000 and you insure it for £10,000 thinking to reduce the premium from £320 a year to £200, what you are also doing is

saying to the insurer 'you underwrite 62.5% of the boat and I shall underwrite 37.5%'.

If you then, say, run into the dock wall, smash the bow, the mast comes down and breaks and you claim the £6,000 it costs to repair the boat and get a new rig, the insurer will be quite entitled to pay you only £3,750 – 62.5% of the claim. Less your £350 excess limit, of course. Averaging will even apply to the costs you have to pay to meet any third party claim – such as the £4,000 the boat next door is claiming because your falling mast brought down their rig.

Third party and limitation of liability

Limitation of liability is a device permitted under the Merchant Shipping Acts whereby an owner of a vessel which is involved in an accident can limit the amount he pays in third-party compensation to a total sum calculated on the size of the vessel. The actual amount varies and is calculated on a somewhat arcane formula involving International Units of Exchange. In the context of insuring sailing cruisers and small boats, the concept seems quite bizarre, a veritable crasher's charter which allows some idiot to wreck your boat and then decline to pay up, but in the context of large vessels the rights of limiting liability, which are agreed under international maritime law, make sense. For many years yacht insurers rarely invoked the right, but more recently the practice has become more common.

Of course, limitation of liability cuts both ways. You (or more correctly your insurer) can use it to limit the amount paid out in respect of any claim against you. Equally, someone who crashes into your boat can use it to avoid having to pay the full cost of repairing your boat. That in itself is a very good reason for having your own insurance, for limitation of liability applies only to third-party claims. It does not enable your insurer to limit how much he will pay you to have your insured boat repaired.

Some years ago, the formula that was used for big ships was used pro rata for yachts, which resulted in some cases in quite ludicrous and manifestly unjust settlement of claims. That has changed and now (2003) the effect of the limitation provision is to allow a yacht owner (or his insurers) to limit liability for third-party property damage to about £60,000, and for death or personal injury to about £120,000. However, limitation does not always apply in every circumstance.

An increasing number of harbour boards and navigation authorities are imposing third-party insurance requirements, and in some cases attempting to exclude the limitation provisions of the Acts, while many boatyards and marinas also insist that their customers have third-party cover. In this context an important aspect of the cover provided is the cost of raising and removing the wreck of an insured boat in the event of it sinking in the fairway of a harbour or marina, or in the main channel of a navigable river or canal.

Betterment

Betterment is a concept you will not come across when buying your first sailing cruiser – but you may well run into it the first time you have to make a claim for repairs. If your boat is quite old, is damaged under insured circumstances and you have to have it repaired, you may well decide that instead – say – of simply having the hole in the side patched and being content with the best job that can be done of matching the repair to the colour of the topsides, you will at the same time have the entire boat repainted; while instead of just straightening the bent stanchions and pulpit you will have all the old and pitted stainless steel work replaced with new. To you, this may make complete sense if only to disguise the repair. The fact that your boat is now better – and worth more – than before the damage was inflicted

may seem like no more than reasonable compensation for the loss and trouble you have suffered. Your insurers, when presented with the bill, may well feel that the improvements, while convenient, are more than were strictly necessary to repair the damage and invite you to contribute, claiming that 'betterment' has occurred. Their view is that, now that the boat has been repaired, it is better than it was before it was damaged.

This, to most folk, will seem no more than fair where, genuinely, they have taken the opportunity of having the boat in the yard and taken to pieces to have it put back together again and various other faults rectified at the same time. Where boat owners tend to gripe at deductions for betterment is where the betterment has been unavoidable such as in my previous` example: a brand new pulpit, for example, because the old one was too mangled to straighten; or where repainting of the entire boat was the only way to cover the repaired area and blend it in with the rest of the hull. The fact that betterment is unheard of in motor insurance, where if someone smashes your old, cracked and faded bumper, you get a smart new one as a matter of course, just makes the pill even harder to swallow.

As in most other things in marine insurance, the answer lies in having a good insurance policy (which is not always and indeed is rarely the cheapest policy) and in negotiating reasonably. Rarely, if ever, is betterment claimed without the insurance company calling in a surveyor or marine loss adjuster to assess both the damage and the work to be done.

The RYA scheme

The RYA has its own marine insurance scheme or, more correctly, one operated for its members on its behalf by a respected insurer, which has been operating successfully since the 1970s. There is, of course, no requirement for RYA members to use this scheme – rather its availability is just one more of the benefits of being a personal member of the RYA. That it is a real benefit may be judged by the fact that when, in 1998, the RNLI (Royal National Lifeboat Institution) decided to promote an insurance scheme for recreational boat owners to offer to its new category of supporter called the RNLI Offshore Member, it could find none better than the already existing RYA scheme, and asked to be allowed to join its name to that. Quite an accolade.

The RYA scheme is operated by the brokers Bishop Skinner & Company Limited (see Appendix 7), and now insures literally thousands of boats, from sailing dinghies to super-yachts. Most of the craft in the scheme are insured either through Northern Star or The Guardian, although for some specialist boats better terms can be found elsewhere. Premiums through the RYA scheme are extremely competitive even before you knock-off the 10% discount for RYA membership, and then further discounts for RYA qualifications – up to 15% for Yachtmaster Offshore.

A particular advantage of using the RYA scheme is that through it the member has available the resources of the RYA Legal Department for the – happily very rare – occasions when claimant and underwriter cannot agree on the settlement of a claim.

1

Registration

In this chapter, 'registration' means registered as a 'British ship', with proper ship's papers, a certificate of registry and an official number on one of the two registers of British ships available to yacht owners. These are the Part I Register (previously known as The Register of Shipping) and the Part III Register, also known as the Small Ships Register (SSR). Both are now established under the Merchant Shipping Act 1995, and maintained in Cardiff by the Register of Ships and Seamen.

Why bother?

There is no national law in the United Kingdom that requires those who buy a yacht either to acquire a license to own it, or to license the yacht herself. This gloriously British personal freedom is one shared less and less by the citizens of other countries, from France to Spain, from Germany to the United States, from New Zealand to Canada. In all of those countries and in many others it is the law of the land that even small boats must be registered and licensed, and bureaucrats being bureaucrats the world over, that inevitably means taxation. In Britain this is not yet the case.

That being said, it is also the case that most cruising yachts in the UK are registered (which is not the same as licensed) and there are a number of reasons for going through this non-obligatory process.

If you intend to take the yacht out of UK coastal waters you do need to have British registry, both to fulfil the requirements of international law to sail on the high seas, and to fulfil the laws of most of the countries into whose territorial waters you will sail. The 1956 Geneva Convention on the High Seas provides that ships take the nationality of their owners, and that states issue documents which provide evidence of the ship's right to fly the flag of the owner's state while on the high seas (in our case that is outside British territorial waters) or the territorial waters of foreign states. Since a yacht falls within the definition of a ship contained in the UK Merchant Shipping Act 1995, the provisions of the convention apply as much to yachts as to commercial vessels.

There are two ways in which a yacht may be placed on the British Register of Shipping and Seamen, which is a Government office maintained by what is currently (2003) known as the Department of Transport. They involve going on either Part I of the Register, which is the part which lists also merchant ships, or Part III – known as the Small Ships Register or SSR for short.

If you are buying the boat with a marine mortgage, the finance company may require her to be on the Part I Register before they will give you the money, no matter where you intend to cruise. This means that if she is not already registered, you will have to register her yourself. If you are a member of a yacht club entitled to wear a privileged ensign (yet another peculiarly British eccentricity), your yacht will have to be on either the Part I Register or the SSR before your yacht club is permitted to issue the warrant you must carry to show you have permission to wear the ensign on your yacht (in the traditional language of seafaring, you 'fly' a flag but you 'wear' an ensign).

So, notwithstanding that there may be no legal compulsion to do so, you will probably want to register your first sailing cruiser.

The Part III Register

This register, also known as the Small Ships Register or SSR, was established in 1983 to cope with both the substantial costs involved in full (Part I) registration and to clear the backlog of work in the Shipping Registry, where there were so many yachts that were having to go through the same paperwork processing channels as big ships that the channels were becoming seriously clogged. In the eyes of the Geneva Convention and the French or Greek harbourmaster, there is no difference between a yacht on the British SSR and a yacht registered under Part I of the UK Merchant Shipping Act 1995: each is as British and as pukha as the other.

In both practice and in law, however, there are some differences. They stem in the main from the more cursory documentation and the fewer formalities required to register on the SSR than on the Part I Register.

The SSR is a self-registration system – that is to say that you fill in the forms yourself. Although there are penalties for making false statements, there are no independent checks on the information you provide, other than cross-checks once the application goes into the system. Because the SSR does not require documentary proof of title going back in a continuous chain to the boat's birth, it does not provide documentary proof of title. If you buy a boat already on the Small Ships' Register, the possession of an SSR number and certificate does not, of itself, provide proof of title resting in the person offering to sell you the boat. Conversely, if you buy a boat not on the register and then put it on the register yourself, when

you come to sell it the prospective buyer may ask for proof of title from you beyond the boat itself being on the register.

Part I registry, on the other hand, does require evidence of title, going back five years before the date of application and so, conversely, thus provides some evidence of title for buyers and gives you the means of showing title when you come to sell if you buy new and have the boat Part I registered.

There is no requirement, or indeed facility, when registering on the SSR to register a mortgage or other charge against the boat. This means that when you buy a boat with an SSR number, you have no way of knowing (at least through its registry) that there might be a charge such as a mortgage still effective against it; and when you come to sell it you cannot prove by virtue of its registry that you are free and unencumbered to do so.

Those few reservations apart, the SSR provides everything that Part I Registration provides, but for (at the time of writing) £10 for a five-year certificate instead of the £400 or so you might pay to put your boat through the altogether more paper-filled rigours of Part I Registration.

How to get on to the SSR

When the SSR first came into effect, it was administered as a service to recreational boat owners by the RYA. However, it has now been taken over by the Registry of Shipping and Seamen, whose address and telephone number is in Appendix 8. The easiest way to get a form is to telephone and go through the nowadays inevitable maze of recorded messages and button pushing before you reach a charming human. That person will ask for your address, and send you an application form which usually comes within two or three working days. You fill in the form and send it back, along with a cheque for £10. Your registration document comes back to you about two weeks later. It used to be in a pale blue book emblazoned with the

Any British ship has the right to wear the country's national maritime ensign – the plain red ensign of our Merchant Navy. Some yacht clubs have the privilege of having special ensigns: sometimes red with their own distinctive badge, sometimes blue, again with a badge, and in some cases the plain blue ensign of the Royal Fleet Auxiliary. In every case each individual member will need a permit to wear the special ensign, issued by the yacht club on behalf of the Secretary of State for Defence. Photo: Moody, Southampton.

Lion and the Unicorn which in impressive looks alone was worth every penny – now it comes in the form of a single, plastic-laminated card valid for five years. *Sic Transit Gloria*. But it is still worth the minimal cost, and could hardly be simpler.

Part I Registration

The disadvantages of Part I Registration over opting for the simpler SSR are its cost, and greater complexity. However, because Part I

Registration investigates the recent ownership history of the vessel you may be reasonably confident that, at least from the point of view of its provenance, there are no nasty skeletons in the hanging locker of your first sailing cruiser. Equally, when you come to sell, your prospective purchaser will have this assurance and this may help facilitate the sale.

Should your boat be stolen, the fact that she is Part I registered may make it easier for the police (or, more likely, the specialist investigator employed by your insurers) to

63

find her. At the least, should a later 'owner' try to register her, the gap in the provenance will become apparent.

Part I Registration used to be a once-only procedure and valid for the life of the vessel. Now it is, like the SSR, renewable every five years and – again like the SSR – the impressive blue book has been replaced by a laminated card.

Registered tonnage and the measurement survey

In addition to providing documentary evidence of title to the boat going back five years, you will be required to engage a professional surveyor to provide the appropriate measurements and calculate the tonnage for the Register.

It might be possible to combine this measurement survey with a full condition survey, but the two must not be confused. The measurement survey is in fact merely a matter of taking a handful of fairly crude measurements of the overall length of the boat, the interior of the main living space, making an allowance for machinery space and doing a simple calculation to an archaic formula to find the registered tonnage.

Registered tonnage has nothing to do with the weight of the boat, but is derived from an 18th century method of estimating how many tuns of French brandy a ship could carry; it is in fact a crude estimate of the internal volume of the ship which can be used commercially. The tonnage was then used to levy fees such as harbour and light dues on the vessel. If it was crude in the 18th century, you may wonder about its relevance to the modern yacht in the 21st century. But for all the best bureaucratic reasons, its requirements remain for a yacht as they do for a passenger liner or a supertanker. In fact, the process and the calculation are essentially the same – it's just that in the case of the yacht, the complexity of the task is somewhat reduced.

If you watch the surveyor carry out the

tonnage survey and see how simple it is, and then think of how much Part I Registration costs, ancient sayings involving money and old rope may well come to mind (I speak as one who has both paid for and been paid to do measurement surveys). Even the most Thespian of surveyors will have difficulty spinning the task out to more than fifteen minutes or making it look even remotely scientific. The point is, however, that the regulations require a professional surveyor to do the measurement survey and professional surveyors are as entitled as any other to be paid for their time be the task simple or complex. And, in fairness, it must be remembered that having a professional third party visit the boat, for whatever reason, is a most useful way of discouraging so-called ghost or fraudulent registration.

It is for this reason that it might be worthwhile asking the surveyor who does your condition survey (which will be before you buy the boat) to do a measurement survey for tonnage and issue a Carving Note while he is there. Even if he charges the full scale fee for the latter, you could save a bit on his travelling expenses.

The Carving Note

The outcome of the measurement survey is the Carving Note. A condition of Part I Registration is that a wood or metal plate, carved with the ship's official number and showing her registered tonnage, be secured to the main beam (the beam under the deckhead aft of the mast) or, in a steel or glassfibre boat, an equivalent position. The Carving Note (the name being another reminder of the arcane origins of this expensive ritual)

(Opposite) *If you are a member of a club which is entitled to wear a so-called privileged ensign, your little ship must be registered and the club secretary must issue a warrant which you must ensure you keep with you when you wear the special ensign. (Note that you fly a signal, a flag or a burgee – but you wear an ensign.)*

CERTIFICATE OF BRITISH REGISTRY

REGISTER OF BRITISH SHIPS PART III
The Merchant Shipping Act 1995
The Merchant Shipping (Registration of Ships) Regulations 1993, as amended
This Certificate is not proof of legal ownership

DATE OF EXPIRY (DD-MM-YYYY)	REGISTRATION NUMBER
27/10/2008	SSR85935

DETAILS OF SHIP
DESCRIPTION: **SAILING YACHT**

OVERALL LENGTH: **7.01 Metres**

NAME OF SHIP: **SPELLBOUND**

NUMBER OF HULLS: 1

HULL ID NUMBER: 64

DETAILS OF REGISTERED OWNERSHIP
MALCOLM ROWLES MCKEAG
SUSAN MARIE MCKEAG

I, the undersigned acting on behalf of the Secretary of State, hereby certify that the details of the ship and registered ownership listed on this Certificate are in accordance with the Register of British Ships Part III (Small Ships Register). This Certificate is valid from:

DATE 23/04/2003

MSF 4706 Rev 9/02
For and on behalf of the Registrar General of Shipping & Seamen
by the Maritime & Coastguard Agency, an Executive Agency of the Government of the United Kingdom

Notes

Renewal or Re-registration
This registration may be renewed for a further period of five years by the person registered as the owner during the three months prior to the date of expiry, provided the details on the Certificate Of Registry have not changed. If any of these details are changed, the registration of the ship will terminate immediately. The ship may however be re-registered, as may a ship for which the Certificate Of Registry has expired. In either case, the present registration number will be retained.

Application Forms
A renewal application will be sent to you prior to the expiry of the current registration. Application forms may be obtained from the address below.

Offences
It is an offence for any person to:
1. with intent to deceive, use or lend or allow to be used by another a Certificate Of Registry whether in force or not;
2. fail to ensure the requirements of ship's marking is met; or
3. fail to surrender a Certificate Of Registry when required by the regulations.

Notification of Change of Address
If you change address, please notify the Register Of British Ships Part III (Small Ships Register) at the address below.

Notification of Sale or Transfer
If the ship is sold or transferred to persons other than those recorded on the Certificate Of Registry, then the registration is terminated and the Certificate must be returned by the registered owner to the address below, along with your confirmation that ownership has been transferred.

Small Ships Register Address
Registry Of Shipping & Seamen, PO Box 420, Cardiff, CF24 5XR. (Telephone: 029 20448855)

PERMIT
By virtue of the Warrant from the Secretary of State for Defence dated **8·2·85** who in pursuance of the authority vested in him under the provisions of Section 73 of the Merchant Shipping Act 1894 has deemed it expedient to authorise Yachts belonging to members of the _____

ROYAL THAMES YACHT CLUB

_____ to wear the **BLUE** _____ Ensign with the distinctive marks thereon* of the aforesaid ~~Squadron~~, Club, ~~Association~~,* the Flag Officers and Committee do hereby authorise the said Ensign to be worn on board the yacht

SPELLBOUND

(registered number _____ **85935** _____)

owned or chartered by **MR. M.R. McKEAG**
a member of the aforesaid ~~Squadron~~, Club, Association* under the conditions printed on the reverse.
This permit shall at all times be revocable at the discretion of the Flag Officers and Committee but is otherwise valid until:* _____ so long as the conditions of issue are fulfilled.

_____ (Signed) **7 January 1999** (Date)

On behalf of the Flag Officers
and Committee.
*Delete where not applicable   Serial No. **22268**

CONDITIONS GOVERNING THE ISSUE OF YACHT PERMITS TO MEMBERS OF ENTITLED YACHT CLUBS IN THE UNITED KINGDOM AND THE CHANNEL ISLANDS

By Section 73 of the Merchant Shipping Act 1894, it is an offence to hoist on board any ship or boat belonging to any British subject certain colours, flags and pendants without a Warrant from Her Majesty the Queen or from the Secretary of State for Defence. The maximum penalty is one thousand pounds for each offence. Among the prohibited flags are the Union Flag, the White Ensign, the Blue Ensign (plain or defaced) and the Red Ensign with any defacement. The prohibition applies to any ship or boat belonging to any British subject wherever it may be, and so extends not only to tidal waters but equally to rivers, lakes and inland waters generally.

Yachts may not wear the special Ensigns prohibited above except:

a. under a Warrant issued to the yacht owner by the Secretary of State for Defence prior to 1 April 1985 and in accordance with the Conditions stated thereon or

b. under a Permit issued to a yacht owner by a Yacht Club from 1 April 1985 onwards and in accordance with the Conditions set out below.

Conditions
1. **Permit.** The Yacht must be issued with a Permit by a Yacht Club pursuant to the granting of a Warrant to that Club by the Secretary of State for Defence.

2. **Registration and Measurement.**
a. **Registration.** The Yacht must be a ship registered under either:
(1) Part of the Merchant Shipping Act 1894; or
(2) The Merchant Shipping Act 1983.
b. **Measurement.** The Yacht must measure not less than:
(1) 2 tons gross if registered under a(1) above.
(2) 7 metres in length overall if registered under a(2) above.

3. **Membership of Designated Yacht Club.** The owner or owners of the Yacht must have current membership of one of the Yacht Clubs in the United Kingdom or Channel Islands to which a Warrant has been issued and which is designated in the Navy list.

4. **Nationality.** The owner or owners must be British subjects.

5. **Use of Yacht.**
a. The special Ensign may only be worn on a Yacht used exclusively for private and personal purposes of the Yachtsman to whom the Permit is issued.
b. The Yacht must not be used for any professional, business or commercial purpose. A Yacht whose name incorporates a name, product or trademark used for business or commercial purpose is not eligible for a Permit.
c. A Yacht which is never used for cruising, e.g. a houseboat, is ineligible for a Permit.

6. **Limited Companies.** A Yacht which is the property of a Limited Company may be eligible for a Permit provided the provisions of Condition 5 are complied with, and the user is a British subject and a member of a designated Yacht Club.

7. **Presence of Holder of Permit.** Except under the provisions of Condition 6, a Permit does not confer any authority while the Yacht is being sailed by anyone other than the owner in person. Thus a special Ensign may not be worn unless the owner or user (see Condition 8) of the Yacht is on board, or in effective control of her when she is in harbour or at anchor near the shore, and the Club's burgee is flown at the main masthead, or other suitable position. The Permit must always be carried on board when a special Ensign is worn.

8. **Separate Authorisation from each Club.** If the owner or user belongs to more than one of the designated Clubs, he must have on board the Permit authorising the particular Ensign which is being worn.
Note – A member of a privilege club who shares a yacht with joint owners ineligible to belong to that club because of restrictive membership qualifications may exceptionally apply for a warrant. All applications under this exception must be supported by written confirmation that the other owners are ineligible for membership of the yacht club concerned. A warrant issued in these circumstances is valid only when the joint owner in whose name the warrant is issued is on board, or in effective control of the yacht when in harbour or at anchor near the shore.

9. **Charter or Loan of Yacht for which Permit issued.** When a Yacht for which a Permit has been issued to a member of a designated Yacht Club is occasionally, and for a short period, let out on charter, such action will not be held to infringe Condition 5 and will not lead to permanent disqualification. However, the Permit must be withdrawn by the Secretary of the Club who shall forthwith cancel it.

10. **Return of Permit.** When a Yacht is sold, there is a change of ownership, or the owner ceases to be a member of the Club, the Permit must at once be surrendered to the Secretary of the Club who shall forthwith cancel it.

11. **Alterations to Permits.** No alterations are to be made to Permits. If the name of the Yacht is changed, or alterations are made which affect the register, the Permit is to be withdrawn by the Secretary of the Club. A new Permit may be issued provided the provisions of these Conditions are otherwise satisfied.

12. **Permits Lost or Stolen.** In the event of a Permit being lost or stolen, the member must forward to the Secretary of the Club a report on the circumstances of the loss and the steps taken to recover it. The Secretary of the Club may, at his discretion, issue a fresh Permit.

13. **Tenders.** The special Ensign may be worn by any boat which belongs to the Yacht and can conveniently be hoisted on board her.

14. **Foreign Cruises.** When cruising in foreign waters a Yacht for which a Permit to wear a special Ensign has been issued should take care to avoid any action which might result in complications with a Foreign Power. To this end, members intending to visit foreign waters affected by war or serious disturbances must give particulars of their voyages to the Secretary of the Club, who should immediately inform the Ministry of Defence (Naval Law Division), Whitehall, London SW1A 2HB.

15. A Permit for a Yacht to wear a special Ensign becomes invalid if the provisions of the above Conditions are not met.

16. **Etiquette.** Permit holders may wish to comply with the custom, when in harbour, of hoisting the Ensign at 0800 (0900 between 1 November and 14 February) and lowering the Ensign at sunset (or 2100 local time if earlier).

gives you the excuse to reach for the Nauticalia catalogue and get yourself one of those nice teak boards carved with the official number and tonnage (quaintly expressed in units and tenths) of your ship. Or rather it will once the remainder of the forms, and the registration fee, have been sent to the Register of Ships and Seamen and you have been issued with the number.

The cost

In 2003 the total cost of Part I Registration was around £450 including the £130 registration fee and the fees and travelling expenses of the surveyor required to do the measurement survey. The RYA has a list of Tonnage Measurers who are qualified to perform this task (drawn in the most part from the ranks of the RYA Technical Division's class measurers, who measure racing boats for compliance with their class rules) and of course any qualified yacht surveyor is also recognised. In 2003 the RYA fee was £20 per hour (with a minimum of £20), plus any travelling expenses involved. A YBDSA surveyor costs £150 (plus expenses) for a boat under 15m, and £195 (plus expenses) for a boat over 15m but under 24m.

Until 1993 Part I Registration was a once-only task. The difficulty with this was that yachts (and ships) once on the register were never taken off. In 1993 the regulations were changed to make Part I the same as the SSR, that is renewable every five years. The entire renewal was done automatically in 1994, making 1999 the year in which the entire Part I Register was due to be updated – a Herculean task for the staff at the Registry, but one which was hoped would reduce the number of yachts and pleasure craft lying on the register from about 45,000 to somewhere around 20,000. Realising the enormity of the task imposed upon the Registry staff, the government brought in special regulations spreading the re-registration task over five years.

Buying a boat already registered

Of course, if the boat you are buying is what is now called 'previously owned' she may well already be on either the SSR or the Part I Register. If the former, the registration is immediately invalidated and you must re-register her – however the form will ask you for details of the previous owner and her previous number of the SSR, so you should make sure you get these with the rest of the ship's papers.

If she is on the Part I Register you simply contact the Registry and transfer ownership to you, providing the necessary documentary evidence of the sale. If, however, the person from whom you are buying the boat did not take the trouble to re-register the yacht in his own name when he originally acquired it, you can have a problem. Assuming there are no questions over the provenance of his title to the boat, you still have to trace the original registered owner to persuade him to sign the Bill of Sale in his favour. If this proves impossible (as is quite likely) you will either have to wait five years before re-registering the boat in your name, or make a formal application to the High Court for an order requiring the Registrar to transfer the title. This, it need hardly be added, could prove expensive as well as time-consuming.

An advantage of buying a boat that is already on the Part I Register is that you will readily know if there are outstanding charges, such as a mortgage. Conversely, because the Small Ships Register does not offer the facility for charges against the boat to be registered, an SSR number is of itself no proof at all that the boat is unencumbered. In the heady days of the 1980s when finance houses seemed to stumble over themselves to lend money, there were a number of cases of unregistered mortgages being offered, it has to be said, to people at whom a more prudent lender would have raised an altogether more quizzical eyebrow. When, inevitably, these less than entirely solid citizens hit financial overfalls in the 1990s, they sold their boats and did not always tell the buyer the entire financial story. The unhappy buyers then found themselves having to deal with finance companies who were still owed money and who had a mortgage charge against the boat. Not for the first time the unwary buyer found morality on his side, but not the law, and some buyers lost many thousands of pounds.

Boatmark Scheme

In 1995, in response to numerous cases of finance fraud, and also to discourage the theft of yachts and yacht equipment, the British Marine Federation set up the Boatmark scheme in collaboration with HPI. HPI is the commercial company which runs the anti-fraud database for the motor trade and has something like 20 million vehicles in its various motor car schemes, so its expertise is considerable.

The Boatmark scheme is based on the Hull Identification Number (HIN) introduced by the BMF in the mid-80s to provide every boat in the country with a unique identifying code number. Each boat originally had its number clearly marked on the transom, either during construction or at one of over a hundred marking stations around the country. The scheme has since been relaunched in 2001 with an electronic tagging system for boats, featuring a unique electronic chip that provides a permanent form of boat identification. The scheme is supported by the Home Office Chipping of Goods Initiative.

The HIN number becomes the key identifier for the record of that particular boat which Boatmark maintains in a database linked with the Police National Computer. Many leading boatbuilders are now embracing the scheme and installing the chips automatically at the manufacturing stage.

The boat's keeper receives a certificate showing details of the boat, the date of first registration, and the name and address of the keeper. When the boat is sold, prospective buyers are able to confirm the validity of the information on the certificate by a simple phone enquiry and sellers have a ready means of demonstrating their craft's background.

Registration under the Boatmark scheme costs (2003) less than £10 to register a boat and all of its equipment due to a subsidy from the Home Office. If you are buying a Boatmarked craft, especially if doing so privately, you can for a modest search fee have Boatmark check the number for you and ensure there are no charges outstanding. Indeed, a Boatmark number will help you check the seller's title to the boat; many police forces are increasingly using Boatmark to report stolen craft.

1

Taking Delivery

Now you have bought the boat, you have to get her to wherever you are going to keep her. If you intend to keep her in the place her previous owner kept her, you have no problems, provided the marina or boatyard are happy to continue looking after her. If you intend to keep her somewhere else, she will need to be moved.

Boatyard sale premiums and other nefarious practices

During the late 1970s and early 1980s, a number of pretty iniquitous practices developed in quite a few boatyards regarding the sale and change of ownership of boats kept at their premises. They got away with it simply because of the excess of demand over supply of berths, while at the same time a number of the more restrictive and one-sided of the practices were fought against by the RYA and others, and most have now largely disappeared.

One such practice that remains in some boatyards is an attempt to secure a slice of the purchase price of any yacht sold out of their premises, no matter by whom owned, how sold, when or to whom. The justification claimed was that the facilities provided by the yard were being used to facilitate the sale, therefore the yard was entitled to a slice of the action; sometimes the practice was enshrined in the berthing or mooring agreement, in which the berth-holder (in this case, the person selling you the boat) had to agree either to use the yard's own brokerage

department to sell the yacht, or pay a proportion of the commission which would have been due on such a sale as compensation if he did not. To some extent this is the seller's problem but it will almost certainly have an impact on the price you are being asked to pay, since the seller will have to build into his asking price the margin the boatyard is demanding.

Another unpleasant practice occasionally which you may come across is where the boatyard, on whose land the boat is stored, demands a special access fee from whomever you employ to deliver the boat to you. If a boatyard runs a delivery service, either by road or by sea, and a boat is sold out of their yard it seems only reasonable that they should expect to be allowed to quote for the job of delivering the boat to her new home. To levy charges in lieu of being given the work seems less reasonable.

One possible way of avoiding such arm-twisting is not to take delivery of the boat at her home port, but at your own, or indeed at some mutually agreed place in between. This way, you avoid having to deal with an unknown boatyard in a distant location handling a boat with which you are unfamiliar. You simply agree with the seller that you will not buy the boat where it is sitting, but you will buy it where you want to keep it. The seller then arranges delivery.

And, of course, even if there is no unpleasant reason to avoid becoming involved with the boatyard where your new boat is stored, from your point of view it is

Since this is your first sailing cruiser and the delivery trip will be your first proper voyage in her, you may find it comforting to employ professional help. It might be a delivery crew or even skipper, or perhaps an instructor from a RYA-recognised sea school, who can both help with the voyage and impart some knowledge and advice. Your adventure is only just beginning. Photo: David Williams.

much more convenient to have the seller arrange delivery. There is also potentially less likelihood of damaging the boat; the existing owner will know of any curious foibles such as where crane slings and the like are supposed to go, while if the sale is not complete until the boat is delivered he will have a strong incentive to supervise the operation properly and ensure that the boat gets to you undamaged.

Road haulage

The simplest way to have the boat delivered is probably by road, provided, of course, that it is possible to get the boat transporter down the little lane to the quiet haven you have chosen. In the event that it is not, you simply have the boat delivered to somewhere easily accessible by road where she can be launched, and then sail her round to her new home.

There are a number of firms who specialise in boat transport. If she is a small boat and is trailable, the problem is relatively easy; with a suitable vehicle you can even collect her yourself. If she is bigger, a specialised low-loader will be needed. Finding a company or individual to deliver your boat by road will be a matter of making some enquiries at the place of delivery, asking the selling broker or yard or just looking in the classified columns of the yachting magazines such as *Yachts and Yachting, Yachting Monthly* or *Practical Boat Owner*.

Of the three, it might be best to start with the yard, marina or yacht club where the boat will be delivered; they can probably recommend someone with whom they deal on a regular basis and whose services they find reliable and competent, and who knows their way of working. Most of the established firms will know the usual places where boats are kept and will have contacts where they have to go to collect your boat. They will also know of any potential difficulties involved in collecting a boat from there, while using a local firm means they are on hand if you have to deal with any problems once it gets there.

Getting her on to the low-loader at the yard where she is to be collected is likely to be a significant part of the cost of the whole operation, especially if she does not sit on her own cradle but on old-fashioned blocks-and-shores which will, of course, belong to the boatyard. You will be liable for the costs of crane hire and labour charges, in addition to the actual deliverey charge. Likewise there will be similar costs at the delivery end.

Naturally, the costs of the delivery will depend on a variety of factors, including the degree of difficulty in handling the boat, the boat's size, the distances involved and the haulier chosen. Transport companies tend to base their charges on the time involved rather than distance and in 1999 a typical delivery charge from a specialist boat transport company was around £450 per day exclusive of lifting charges, and the total cost of transporting a 23-footer from Essex to Hampshire was about £500.

On her own bottom

One option is to sail the boat to her new home. Either you can do it yourself, or employ a delivery skipper and crew.

Doing the delivery yourself means, more or less by definition, taking delivery of the boat at her old home. On the one hand, it is certainly an excellent way to get acquainted with your new joy, and could make an enjoyable and worthwhile first cruise. On the other hand, it might prove to be a most salutary way of getting acquainted with all the

things that need to be done to your new boat before she can be anything approaching a joy, and the first cruise could turn into, at best, a nightmare of breakages, leaks and things going wrong and, at worst, an exercise in emergency survival. On balance, it is probably not advisable to attempt anything more than a very modest delivery trip in your first sailing cruiser, an unknown and, by you at least, untried boat.

One way round the problem might be to recruit a crew of friends who between them have enough experience to cope with unexpected problems and effect extemporaneous solutions. Another is to employ professionals. Unlike sailing schools, which it does recognise (or not, as the case may be), the RYA does not license, register or recommend yacht-crewing agencies, but it does keep an ad hoc list, updated from time to time. Nor does there appear to be any professional body – the equivalent, for example, of the YBDSA for brokers and surveyors – which represents or regulates delivery crews. Probably the best place to look, other than local contacts in the vicinity of where the boat is kept and who are personally known to the seller, the broker or the surveyor with whom you are dealing, are the classified ad sections of *Yachting Monthly* and *Yachting World* magazines, the former (which is a dedicated cruising magazine) in particular.

Whichever method you choose, you must decide how you will take delivery of your first sailing cruiser before you buy her, and the costs of doing so must be put in your budget. Remember, too, to insure the boat properly for whichever method you choose, making sure that she is insured for all the waters and sea areas she will sail through on her passage to her new home.

12

Where to Keep Her?

Perhaps this chapter should have been Chapter 1, for there is little point in buying your first, or indeed any, sailing cruiser if you have not worked out where you will keep her.

Where you keep the boat is inextricably linked to the sort of sailing you want to do on the one hand, and your budget on the other. Will she be:

- Abroad – probably the Mediterranean?
- At home in the UK?
- In a marina, or on a swinging mooring?
- On her trailer at home?
- In a boatyard, ready to launch or roll?

Abroad

Increasingly, many British owners keep their yachts abroad. The Channel and Brittany coasts of France, the Mediterranean and the West Indies are all popular and the option is by no means reserved for the wealthiest. With cheap cross-Channel ferries and Eurostar combined with marina fees a fraction of the cost of those in the United Kingdom, it can actually be cheaper keeping a boat of, say, 35ft (10.6m) in France than in the UK. Cheap flights from Northern and Midland airports to smaller French airports such as Deauville, Dinard and Nantes mean that the attractive possibility of keeping your boat in somewhere like Cherbourg or St Malo is no longer reserved only for those who live on the South Coast. The larger the boat, the greater the saving, since not only do the marina fees themselves continue to compare favourably,

but the 'overhead' costs of getting there become increasingly marginal.

The very wealthy employ 'facility management agents' (a very upscale name for boat captain, if ever there was one) to look after their yachts in places like Monaco, Antibes and the Cote-d'Azur but you and your first sailing cruiser are unlikely to be in that league. Rather, you will probably make an arrangement with a French marina or boatyard, exactly as you would with a marina at home. Nor does the boat have to be as big even as 35ft (10.6m); one Scottish yacht broker has, for years, kept his 22-footer (6.7m) in a yard above the barrage at Dinard and he and his family look forward to family breaks with the happy fervour of devoted and regular pilgrims.

The Mediterranean marinas, from Gibraltar to the Aegean, are positively thick with British-owned boats, and while hot spots such as St Tropez and Puerto Cervo may well be the haunts of those long past owning their first sailing cruiser, places like Palma and Gibraltar have a plentiful sprinkling of Hunters, Westerlies and Moodys whose owners live in the United Kingdom.

Language and currency aside, the principal difference and most likely potential difficulty when deciding to keep your boat abroad lies in documentation, and differing approaches to licensing and regulation. The United Kingdom is one of the least regulated countries of Europe when it comes to boat ownership: others are much more hedged around with bureaucracy.

Where will you keep her? This aerial shot of a marina on the Hamble River shows most of the ways to keep your first sailing cruiser. In the middle of the picture is the marina itself. Just below the marina you can see boats kept on piles owned by the local harbour authority – low in price, but usually with a long waiting list. In the immediate foreground are boats moored to free floating (that is, not attached to the shore) pontoons. These might be owned by a yard, the local authority or even a yacht club. Beside the sheds are boats which are dry-sailed: kept ashore on trailers, and launched only when their owner is ready to go sailing. This is an increasingly popular solution for owners with small sailing cruisers. Each method has its advantages and disadvantages in cost and convenience. In general: the more convenient, the more costly. Photo: Hamble Point Marina, MDL.

The emphasis can vary from country to country; the principal motivation of the paper-checkers in France and Greece would appear to be fiscal, while in the Netherlands and Germany the emphasis appears to be more on the capabilities of boat and crew, but whatever the motives behind the penchant for paper, you as a European citizen must pay heed.

The RYA's Sail Cruising Division has files inches thick on the paperwork required by different countries both for visitors and for those planning on semi-permanent berths, and will advise members on contact.

In the UK

We are fortunate indeed in this country to have such a wide range of options when it comes to the places and manner in which we can keep our sailing cruisers; from swinging moorings on rivers to fully-serviced marinas. True, there tends to be the over-riding consideration of money; and true, a great deal depends on where you live, but by and large we are as well off in this respect as most of our European neighbours, and better off than many.

Marinas

There are currently some 400 marinas and yacht harbours known to the RYA. They range from small 40-berth (or even less) marinas to marinas with berths for several hundred, although there is nothing in the UK to compare with the huge 1,000-plus-berth harbour cities in the United States, such as Fort Lauderdale in Florida. The level of service is as varied as the size and location, from do-it-yourself pontoons to fully-serviced berths with water, electricity and even cable TV.

Marinas got themselves something of a bad reputation in the 1980s, when demand for berths far outstripped supply. It was a seller's market with a vengeance and there were notoriously shameful and nakedly avaricious practices attempted, many of which were successfully fought against by the RYA. Charges soared, unfair contract terms and restrictive practices abounded (one notorious chief executive promised openly to squeeze yachtsmen 'until the pips squeaked') and the greed of what was in fact a minority, albeit a sizeable one and mostly in the south of the country, tarnished the whole industry.

Happily, things are rather different now we are at the turn of the century: the explosive expansion of small boat sailing has slowed, marina berth building has expanded, alternative berthing arrangements and sites have opened up and the market has balanced. No less significantly, boat owners have accepted that a marina is an expensive place to build and maintain and that trying to compare the cost of keeping the boat in a marina berth with the cost of keeping it on a swinging mooring 30 or 40 years ago is a rather pointless exercise. Most marinas are pleasant and friendly places to keep your boat, with helpful staff and a degree of convenience that, once you have sampled it, will make you feel very disinclined to try any other arrangement.

That said, a full-service marina berth is still among the more expensive options but you do get a lot of convenience for your money. Like the cost of hotels and for that matter property, marina berth prices vary not only with the level of service but with the location.

There can be surprising anomalies: you might think that one of the most expensive places to keep a boat in Britain would be Cowes, the 'holy city' of south coast yachting. In fact Cowes is one of the more reasonable places, not just for marina charges but for all sailing related services, not least because of the harsh economics of supply and demand on an island detached even by so narrow a moat as The Solent from the main boating population. Permanent berths in Cowes itself are few, and like gold dust, because the main marina is intentionally kept available for visitors and big events, but upriver there is ample parking of all types.

Marina berths tend to be sold on an all-year round basis. Some marinas base their annual charge on so many months afloat, so many months stored ashore. Some include in the annual charge one free lift out and one free launch: others charge separately. Some will require you to provide (or pay them to make) her own cradle if the boat is to sit ashore.

On a mooring

The most popular places for moorings are those which offer shelter, are close to the facilities needed to maintain boats and people, which are easy to get to by road and which offer reasonably quick access to good sailing water. Given such a list of requirements it is not hard to see why places like the Hamble on the south coast, or the Gareloch on the Clyde, are among Britain's longest-established yachting centres. There are, of course, many others.

You can still find a place where a friendly farmer will let you put down your own mooring at the bottom of a lane running down to a river, and a local longshoreman

The simple swinging mooring, although still the simplest and among the cheapest of ways of mooring a small sailing boat, is becoming increasingly rare especially in popular yachting centres, squeezed out by marinas, pontoons and crowded piles. You will, of course, need a means of getting out to the boat: your own tender, yacht club or yard launch. Photo: David Williams.

will keep his eye on the boat for you when you are not there, but you have to be very lucky. (The next piece of advice about such a place must surely be – when you find it, tell not a soul.)

Most moorings tend to be operated by a body such as a boatyard, a harbour authority, a local council or a yacht club. Of these, the most expensive, not unnaturally, are those operated commercially by commercial yards. Like marina berths, the price can depend as much upon location as on any other factor.

In many harbours and on many rivers, particularly in England, the local harbour authority either owns or leases from (usually) the Crown Estate the river-bed ground on which it then puts down moorings. The cost of such moorings depends as much on the political (with a small 'p') stance and status of

the authority as it does on locality and commerce. The Crown Estate policy was changed, by the Thatcher government, from regarding such use of its land as an amenity for society to regarding it as a commercial resource to be sold for as much as the market would stand. However, many if not most harbour authorities, being set up as independent statutory bodies, still accept that boating is a healthy and worthwhile pastime indulged by a broad cross-section of the community and thus regard the provision of mooring facilities as an amenity for the town or area, rather like the provision of football pitches, recreation grounds and car parks. Indeed, many harbour authorities are prevented by their constitutions from making a profit from any of the services they provide and are required by law to provide them as amenities.

The Bristol Harbour Festival is a great opportunity for sailors to get together with a group of like-minded people, swop sea stories and enjoy the local culture. Photo: David Williams.

The result is that there is often quite a large difference in the cost of a commercial mooring and the cost of a municipal mooring even on the same river or harbour. There is also usually quite a long waiting list. Some local authorities limit availability of their moorings to local residents – a practice as stoutly protected by the locals as it is roundly condemned by those who live in the middle of the country and fail to see by what right those who live close to the coast should think they may thus arrogate its use to themselves.

If you keep your boat on a river governed by some sort of local authority, there will be some sort of licence fee to pay. This will vary, often widely and wildly, from place to place. On the Medway, for example, the local authority licence for a 30ft (9m) boat is £147.75 (2003) for an annual licence on top of the mooring fee, while on the Lymington

River in Hampshire the Harbour Commissioner's fee is subsumed into the overall mooring fee which is not a great deal more, provided you have waited the ten years or so it currently takes to get one.

Some yacht clubs operate moorings as a service to their members. Like municipal moorings, they are usually costed on an amenity rather than profit-making basis and thus, like municipal moorings, often have quite lengthy waiting lists. Sometimes the yacht club rents the moorings from the local authority. They might be swinging moorings, pile moorings or even in some cases the yacht club does a deal to park a floating pontoon in the river or harbour, and then sub-lets the space alongside to its members. In other cases, the yacht club has been able to develop its own land, putting in moorings or even, in one or two celebrated and (for the members) most happy cases, being able to build their own private marina. Naturally, such a facility is both a tremendous benefit to members and a considerable draw for new members. You will usually find, if you wish to join such a club so as to avail yourself of a cheap marina berth, that there is both a waiting list for berths and a club rule that one must have been a member for so many years before your name even goes into the hat.

Something you must bear in mind if you elect to keep your boat on any sort of mooring, unconnected to the shore, is the means of getting out to the boat. You may need to buy yourself some sort of tender or dinghy and find somewhere to store it securely. Even if you are using a yacht club mooring or a yard mooring and there is a club or yard launch service, this will normally operate only at certain times. If you come down to the boat outside those times, you will not be able to get out to her; if you are away from your mooring and come back outside those times you may find yourself marooned on your boat, unless you have made your own independent arrangements.

Keep her at home

If your first sailing cruiser is a little trailer-sailer, you might keep her on her trailer at home. In addition to making sure you have room to do so, you need to make sure there will be no insurmountable objections from either the neighbours, or the local authority.

In the 1970s there was a celebrated attempt by the Greater Manchester Council to introduce to Parliament what became known as the Boats In Gardens Bill – an extension of the Council's planning powers so as to require any householder wishing to keep a boat on their own driveway to seek planning permission from the Council before being allowed to do so. Even worse were the powers sought by the Council to allow them to say 'no' to such a modest and reasonable request. The RYA mounted a vigorous campaign to defeat this basic intrusion upon boat-owners' rights, and won. The decision set a precedent and since then, thanks to this landmark campaign, you should find few if any restrictions to park your own boat in your own back garden or, more likely, driveway.

Appendix 1

Terms of Agreement for Construction of a New Craft

Agreement for the Construction of a New Boat

Build Number/Hull Identification No./Boatmark No.

THIS AGREEMENT is made the day of

BETWEEN

1. [   ] a limited company incorporated in England (Reg.no. No.)/ Scotland (Reg.no. No.)/Northern Ireland (Reg.no. No.)/a sole trader/a partnership whose registered office/principal place of business is [   ] ("the Builders")

AND

2. [   ] of [   ] "The Purchaser"

(jointly "the Parties")

1 Agreement and Specification of the Boat

1.1 The Builders agree to construct and the Purchaser agrees to buy the boat described in the Specification as set out in Schedule 1, together with any drawings and plans, all of which shall be signed by the Parties, ("the

Boat") and in accordance with the terms of this Agreement.

1.2 Subject to any agreed amendments to the Specification, drawings and plans, the Purchaser shall have the right to reject any workmanship, materials and/or equipment which does not comply therewith. Such rejection shall be ineffective unless confirmed to the Builders by notice in writing within 14 days.

1.3 The Builders shall be under no contractual or other obligation to accept any order of the Purchaser until it has been confirmed and signed on behalf of the Builders by their authorised representative.

1.4 The Builders shall build the Boat in compliance with all applicable statutory requirements and regulations relating to the construction and sale of the Boat in the European Union or any other requirements or regulations which may be agreed in writing between the Parties.

2 Modifications and Changes to the Specification

2.1 No modifications or changes to the Specification, Delivery Date and/or price shall be binding on the Parties unless and until set out in writing and signed by both Parties.

2.2 The Builders shall have the right to refuse

to agree to any modification or change to the Specification or Plans.

3 Contract Price and Payment

3.1 The price of the Boat is the amount set out in Schedule 2 together with the cost of any modifications or changes to the Specification agreed between the Parties under Clause 2.1 and any adjustments made under Clause 3.3 and, if applicable, VAT at the rate applicable from time to time (together "the Contract Price"). The Purchaser agrees to pay the Contract Price by instalments as set out in Schedule 2 ("Stage Payments") and as provided in this Clause.

3.2 The Builders shall give the Purchaser 14 days' notice of the anticipated date of completion of each stage of construction as provided in Schedule 2. On expiry of such notice the Purchaser shall certify that the stage has been satisfactorily completed (such certification not to be unreasonably withheld) whereupon the relevant Stage Payment will become immediately due and payable in full without discount, deduction or set off.

EITHER - Delete one of the alternatives to Clause 3.3 (see Notes for Guidance)

3.3 If during the period of this Agreement there is an increase in the Builders' net costs of constructing the Boat, whether in relation to materials or labour or which arises from any change in the applicable law or regulations, and provided always that the Builders have proceeded with reasonable despatch, the Parties agree that the Builders shall be entitled to increase the Contract Price proportionately to such increase in cost and the Purchaser undertakes and agrees to pay the Contract Price as so adjusted.

OR

3.3 Save as provided in Clauses 2.1 and 3.1

the Contract Price shall not be subject to any increase.

3.4 If the Contract Price is varied in accordance with Clauses 2.1 and/or 3.1 the Builders shall be entitled to require payment of any increase in the Contract Price by reason of any modification or change in full at the time of agreement thereto or, at their option, to receive such increase by way of additions to the Stage Payments.

3.5 If the Contract Price is varied in accordance with Clause 3.3 the amount of the increase shall be divided by the number of remaining Stage Payments and the amount so calculated shall be added to each remaining Stage Payment and Schedule 2 shall be amended accordingly.

3.6 If for any reason any tax, levy, charge or any other sum required to be paid by law shall be omitted from the amount of the Contract Price or shall be varied or introduced after the date of this Agreement and shall be required to be paid by the Purchaser the Purchaser shall pay such additional sum forthwith on demand.

4 Unpaid Installments

4.1 If the Purchaser fails for any reason to pay the full amount of any Stage Payment or other sum due to the Builders on the due date the Builders shall be entitled to stop construction of the Boat until all outstanding payments have been paid in full, and the Delivery Date shall be extended by the period of such delay in payment.

4.2 If such failure to pay any sum due continues for 14 days the Builders shall thereafter be entitled to charge interest at 4% over Barclays Bank plc base rate, or the Builders' current commercial overdraft rate if higher, after as well as before judgement, calculated from the date upon which such payment became due and payable.

4.3 After a further period of 14 days' delay the Builders shall, without prejudice to any other rights, be entitled:

4.3.1 to require payment from the Purchaser forthwith of the balance of the Contract Price then outstanding and to complete the construction of the Boat; or

4.3.2 to terminate this Agreement and to sell the Boat pursuant to Clause 10.2.

4.4 The Purchaser shall in addition be liable for any loss or damage, special, direct, indirect and/or consequential losses incurred by the Builders as a result of the delay in the payment of the Stage Payments or any other sums due hereunder.

5 Acceptance Trial and Delivery

5.1 The Boat shall be completed and ready for delivery at the place and on the date stated in Schedule 3 or on such later date as may be determined in accordance with the terms of this Agreement ("the Delivery Date").

5.2 Unless otherwise agreed between the Parties the Boat shall at the Builders' expense be taken on a trial trip (of not more than [   ] hours' duration) before delivery (the "Acceptance Trial"). The Builders shall give the Purchaser at least 14 days' written notice of the place and approximate duration of the Acceptance Trial, but if the date shall not be convenient to the Purchaser the Parties shall agree an alternative date not more than one month after the date proposed by the Builders.

5.3 If during the Acceptance Trial any defects in workmanship or materials or deviations from the Specification are found, the Builders shall forthwith rectify such defects or deviations and shall carry out a further Acceptance Trial in accordance with Clause 5.2.

5.4 If the Purchaser fails to attend a first Acceptance Trial, the Builders shall carry out a further Acceptance Trial pursuant to Clause 5.2, save that the cost thereof shall be for the account of the Purchaser.

5.5 If the Purchaser fails to attend such further Acceptance Trial, or if the Parties shall fail to agree an alternative date for a first or further Acceptance Trial, the Builders shall confirm in writing to the Purchaser that an Acceptance Trial has been deemed to have taken place and provided that the Builders shall certify that the Boat is constructed in accordance with the Specification and performs satisfactorily the Purchaser shall be deemed to have accepted it.

5.6 At the satisfactory conclusion of the Acceptance Trial the Purchaser shall sign the Certificate of Delivery and Acceptance in the form provided in Schedule 4. The final balance of the Contract Price shall become due and payable immediately upon signature of the Certificate of Delivery and Acceptance or upon provision by the Builders to the Purchaser of the Certificate referred to at Clause 5.5 or upon the Purchaser's wrongful failure or refusal to sign the Certificate of Delivery and Acceptance.

5.7 The Purchaser shall take delivery of the Boat immediately upon signature by the Purchaser of the Certificate of Delivery and Acceptance and payment of the final balance of the Contract Price and any other sums owing to the Builders by the Purchaser. If the Purchaser fails to take delivery of the Boat or fails to pay any outstanding sums due to the Builders then, in addition to any other rights which the Builders may have, the Builders shall be entitled to require the Purchaser to pay such reasonable berthing and/or storage charges as the Builders shall notify to the Purchaser together with any other expenses reasonably incurred by the Builders, including but not limited to insurance, maintenance and lifting of the Boat in or out of the water until actual delivery shall take place.

5.8 The Purchaser and the Builders expressly agree that the Builders shall not be responsible for investigating or otherwise ensuring that the Purchaser is competent and experienced in the proper control and/or navigation of the Boat. The Royal Yachting Association will if requested by the Purchaser provide a list of boat handling/training establishments.

6 Delays and Extensions of Time (Force Majeure)

6.1 If construction of the Boat is delayed directly or indirectly due to any cause beyond the Builders' reasonable control the Delivery Date shall be extended by the period of time during which such delaying event operates.

6.2 The Builders shall give the Purchaser written notice of any event in respect of which the Builders claim to be entitled to an extension of time:

6.2.1 within 7 days of its commencement, stating the date on which the delay commenced, the cause of it and its estimated duration; and

6.2.2 within 7 days of its end, stating the date on which it ended and the total period of the extension sought.

Any dispute arising between the Parties as to the operation of a delaying event shall be adjudicated in accordance with Clause 14.1.

6.3 If the Builders' premises, plant, machinery or equipment shall be so damaged by the operation of a delaying event for which the Builders are not responsible so as to make it impracticable for the Builders to complete the construction of the Boat, the Builders may, at their option (to be exercised within 21 days of

the operation of the delaying event), cancel this Agreement by notice in writing to the Purchaser, whereupon the Purchaser shall be entitled by written election either:

6.3.1 to take over and complete the Boat without further liability on the Builders whereupon the Purchaser shall pay to the Builders all sums then due, whether by way of Stage Payments or otherwise; or

6.3.2 to require repayment of all instalments paid by the Purchaser to the Builders and upon such repayment title in the Boat and all materials and equipment appropriated to the Boat shall revest in the Builders.

7 Access to Boat and to Builders Premises

7.1 The Purchaser shall have the right to inspect the progress of construction of the Boat from time to time during the Builders' normal business hours with the prior written consent of the Builders, such consent not to be unreasonably withheld provided always that the Builders shall be entitled to appoint a representative to accompany the Purchaser or Purchaser's agent and that access shall extend only to those parts of the Builders' premises necessary for the inspection of the Boat and/or the materials and equipment appropriated thereto.

7.2 The Purchaser shall observe all current rules and regulations applied by and to the Builders, and to their premises.

8 Warranties

In addition to the Purchaser's statutory rights the following warranties shall apply:

8.1 Subject to the conditions set out below and otherwise expressly set out herein the Builders warrant to the Purchaser that the Boat will be of satisfactory quality and reasonably fit for the purpose(s) made known to the Builders in writing prior to the date of this Agreement whether or not such purpose is one for which the Boat is commonly supplied and will correspond with the Specification and any variation, addition or modification thereto. The Builders further warrant that the Boat will be free from defects in materials and workmanship for a period of 12 months from the time of delivery.

8.2 The Builders warrant to the Purchaser that on delivery the Boat will comply with:

8.2.1 all legislative requirements and regulations relating to the sale of the Boat in the European Union for any purpose(s) made known under 8.1 above; or

8.2.2 any other requirements or regulations which may be agreed in writing between the Parties.

8.3 The Purchaser's statutory rights and the warranties set out in Clauses 8.1 and 8.2 shall be subject to the following conditions:

8.3.1 The Builders shall have no liability for any defect in the Boat arising from the Specification supplied, provided or varied by the Purchaser;

8.3.2 The Builders shall repair or replace any defect in the workmanship, materials or equipment or their failure to correspond with the Specification. Such repair or replacement shall be carried out by the Builders at their premises or, where that is not convenient to the Parties, the Builders shall pay the reasonable cost of having the work carried out elsewhere;

8.3.3 The Builders shall only be liable for any defects or failures which were not apparent on reasonable inspection during the Acceptance Trial or within a reasonable time thereafter;

8.3.4 The Purchaser shall notify the Builders

in writing immediately on discovery of any alleged defect and the Builders or their agent shall have the right to inspect the Boat including the right to carry out sea trials to enable the Builders or their agent to examine or assess the extent of the alleged defect. The expense of any such trials shall be borne by the Builders if the defect is shown to be one of workmanship or materials.

9 Insurance

9.1 The Builders shall insure the Boat (together with all equipment and materials installed or intended for it and within the Builders' premises) in the joint names of the Builders and the Purchaser from the date of this Agreement until the date of delivery.

9.2 Such insurance shall be effected with a reputable insurer for a sum equal to the replacement cost of the completed Boat (to a maximum of 125% of the Contract Price) and shall include the cost of any additions or variations to the Specification which have been agreed between the Parties.

9.3 Such insurance shall be on terms no less favourable than the Institute Clauses for Builders' Risks applicable from time to time. Documentary evidence of such insurance, its terms and conditions and proof of payment of the premium shall be provided to the Purchaser on request.

9.4 In the event that the Boat, equipment or materials sustain damage at any time before delivery any monies received in respect of the insurance shall be receivable by the Builders and shall be applied by them in making good such damage in a reasonable and workmanlike manner and the Delivery Date shall be extended by such period as shall be reasonably necessary to effect the necessary repairs. The Purchaser shall not be entitled to reject the Boat, equipment or materials on account of such damage or repairs or to make any claim in respect of any resultant depreciation save that where the Boat is declared an actual or constructive total loss the Purchaser shall have the option, to be exercised within 28 days of the loss, of cancelling this Agreement in which event the insurance money to the value of Stage Payments already paid shall be paid direct to the Purchaser by the insurers and the Purchaser will abandon all rights under the said insurance to the Builders. This Agreement will thereupon be determined in all respects as if it had been duly completed and the Purchaser shall have no further right to claim against the Builders.

9.5 If the Builders fail to provide satisfactory evidence of insurance in accordance with the provisions of this Clause, the Purchaser shall be entitled to insure on comparable terms and to deduct the amount of the premium actually paid from the Contract Price.

10 Termination

10.1 The Builders shall be entitled to terminate this Agreement by written notice without prejudice to any other rights or remedies available if:

10.1.1 the Purchaser becomes insolvent; or

10.1.2 the Purchaser has failed without good reason to make one or more Stage Payments or any other payment within 28 days of such payment being due and payable and has not referred the underlying reason for such delay to dispute resolution under the provisions of Clause 14.

10.2 If the Builders exercise their right to terminate this Agreement under Clause 10.1 they shall be entitled to sell the Boat, the materials and the equipment and/or any other property of the Purchaser in the possession of the Builders for the purpose of the construction of the Boat. The Builders shall give the Purchaser 28 days' written notice of their intention to sell the Boat

and/or other property and such notice shall give details of the reasons for the sale including details of any sums due and payable to the Builders together with details of the proposed method of sale. Following the sale of the Boat and/or other property the Builders shall repay to the Purchaser the balance of the proceeds of sale after deduction of all sums owing to the Builders and all reasonable legal or other expenses including, but not limited to, the costs of sale and maintenance and storage charges incurred by the Builders.

10.3 In addition to any other rights set out herein the provisions of the Torts (Interference with Goods) Act 1977 ("the Act") shall apply in relation to uncollected boats and/or other property and for the purposes of the Act it is hereby expressly agreed that the Builders' obligations to the Purchaser as custodians of the Boat and/or other property terminate upon the expiry or lawful termination of this Agreement and pursuant to the Act the Builders have a right of sale exercisable in certain circumstances as set out in the Act.

10.4 For the purposes of Clauses 10.2 and 10.3 only the Purchaser hereby irrevocably appoints the Builders as the agent of the Purchaser for the sale of the Boat and/or other property. The Purchaser shall co-operate with the Builders insofar as may be necessary to effect a sale of the Boat including signing or confirming any authority or instructions.

11 Ownership of the Boat

11.1 The Boat and/or all materials and equipment purchased or appropriated from time to time by the Builders specifically for its construction (whether in their premises, upon the water or elsewhere) shall become the property of the Purchaser upon the payment of the first Stage Payment or, if later, upon the date of the said purchase or appropriation. The Builders shall, however, have a lien on the Boat and any materials or equipment purchased for or appropriated to the construction for recovery of all sums due (whether invoiced or not) under the terms of this Agreement or any variation or modification hereof. Any materials or equipment rejected by the Purchaser shall forthwith revest in the Builders.

11.2 The Builders shall, insofar as it is reasonably practicable to do so, mark all individual items of equipment and materials which are purchased for or appropriated to the construction of the Boat.

11.3 The Purchaser shall not without the prior written consent of the Builder which consent shall not be unreasonably withheld sell, assign, pledge or otherwise put a charge on the Boat by way of security for any indebtedness prior to delivery except for the sole purpose of obtaining a loan to finance the construction of the Boat. If the Purchaser charges the Boat in breach of the terms of this Clause, the balance of the Contract Price shall forthwith become due and payable without prejudice to any other rights or remedies of the Builders. The Purchaser shall not have the right to assign or transfer this Agreement or any of his rights and obligations hereunder without the prior written consent of the Builders.

11.4 If the Purchaser is in breach of any of the terms of this Agreement after the property in the Boat and/or materials and equipment has passed to him and the Builders wish to exercise their rights to sell the Boat and/or materials and equipment as set out herein then the property in the Boat and/or materials shall revert from the Purchaser to the Builders following 28 days' notice by the Builders of their intention to exercise such rights.

11.5 Notwithstanding the provisions of this Clause risk in the Boat shall remain with the Builders until the actual delivery of the Boat to the Purchaser.

12 Copyright

Any copyright or similar protection in manuals, drawings, plans, specifications, including the Specification prepared by the Builders or their employees or agents, shall remain the property of the Builders.

13 Notices

Any notice required to be given hereunder shall be in writing and either (i) given by hand with proof of delivery or electronic transmission confirmed forthwith by first class pre-paid post, or (ii) sent by first class pre-paid post to the other party at the address set out in this Agreement or such other address in the UK as may have been notified by the other party.

14 Dispute Resolution – Law and Jurisdiction

14.1 If during the construction of the Boat any dispute arises either as to an adjustment of the Contract Price pursuant to Clause 3.3 or as to when a Stage Payment is due and payable or as to the operation or duration of a delaying event or whether for the purposes of the policy of insurance the Boat has suffered substantial damage, then, and without prejudice to the Parties' rights to litigate such dispute, it may be referred to a single surveyor who shall be independent of the Builders and the Purchaser and whose identity and terms of reference shall be agreed by the Parties or, in default of agreement, by the President for the time being of the Yacht Designers and Surveyors Association.

The surveyor so appointed shall act as an expert and not as an arbitrator and his written decision shall be final and binding upon the Parties and his fees and expenses shall be borne equally by the Parties.

14.2 This Agreement shall be construed in accordance with English law or where the Builders have their principal place of business in Scotland in accordance with Scottish law and the High Court of England or Scotland (as the case may be) shall have exclusive jurisdiction in respect of any dispute or other matter arising hereunder.

15 Interpretation

15.1 The construction of this Agreement is not to be affected by any headings.

15.2 References in this Agreement to the Parties shall include their respective successors and permitted assigns save where such succession or assignment is expressly prohibited by the terms of this Agreement.

15.3 This Agreement forms the entire agreement between the Parties and unless specifically agreed in writing by the Builders no warranty, condition, description or representation is given or to be implied by anything said or written in the negotiations between the Parties or their representatives prior to this Agreement.

15.4 If the Builders are a member of a group of companies the Builders may perform any of its obligations or exercise any of its rights hereunder by itself or through any member of its group provided that any act or omission of any such other member shall be deemed to be the act or omission of the Builders.

15.5 In this Agreement words importing the masculine gender also include the neuter and feminine gender and words importing the singular include also the plural.

15.6 Reference to any legislative provision includes a reference to that provision as amended extended or re-enacted and any replacement thereof (either before or after the date of this Agreement).

15.7 If any term or provision in this Agreement shall be held to be void in whole or in part under any enactment or rule of law such term or provision or part shall to that extent be deemed not to form part of this Agreement but the validity and enforceability of the remainder of this Agreement shall not be affected.

16 Variations and Additions

This Agreement is subject to the variations and additions set out below or identified below and attached to this Agreement and initialled and dated by both Parties.

Signed for and on behalf of the Builders

In the presence of:
Full name of witness
Address
Occupation
Signature

Signed for and on behalf of the Purchasers

In the presence of:
Full name of witness
Address
Occupation
Signature

N.B. (1 Witness in England, 2 in Scotland)

Schedule 1 – Specification

The Specification for the Boat is as set out below or as identified below and attached to this Agreement and signed by the Parties.

Schedule 2 – Stage Payments

Contract Price

The Boat £

Plus VAT (if applicable)
£
Price inclusive of VAT
£

The Contract Price shall be payable by Stage Payments as set out below

1) Upon signing of this Agreement £

2) Upon the hull being available at the Builders' premises fully moulded, planked, plated or formed and confirmed in writing to the Purchaser by the Builders
£

3) Upon substantial completion of the fitting of the interior joinery work or installation of the engine or stepping of the mast whichever is the earlier
£

4) Upon completion of the Acceptance Trial and the signing of the Satisfaction Notice by the Purchaser or upon deemed acceptance and completion of the Builders' Certification as provided in Clauses 5.5 and 5.6 £

Schedule 3 – Delivery

Delivery Date
Place of Delivery

Schedule 4 – Certificate of Delivery & Acceptance

Place of Acceptance Trial
Date of Acceptance Trial
Persons present at Acceptance Trial

I the undersigned hereby certify that the construction of the Boat and the Acceptance Trial have been completed to my reasonable satisfaction.

Subject to the terms of the Agreement dated [   ] this Certificate of Delivery and Acceptance will not affect my statutory rights should the Boat or its equipment subsequently prove to be defective.

Signed by [   ], the Purchaser

Dated

Notes

These are explanatory notes only and, although very important, do not form part of the agreement itself.

1. This form is published by the British Marine Industries Federation (BMIF) and approved by the Royal Yachting Association (RYA).

2. It is a simple form of agreement designed for the leisure marine market and cannot be expected to cater for every unforeseen circumstance arising between the parties. It is considered be the RYA and the BMIF to strike a fair balance between the interests of purchaser and the builders. Certain aspects of this agreement can be used for transactions between commercial parties.

3. It should be completed in duplicate, taking care to insert the appropriate details on pages 1 and 2. Any specification, drawing or additional clause which cannot be accommodated on the agreement should be firmly attached to the agreement and signed by both parties. Additional clauses inserted on page 8 should be initialled by both parties.

4. Both parties should sign (in the presence of a witness in Scotland).

5. The Certificate of Delivery and Acceptance must be signed by the purchaser or his agent on delivery and acceptance of the completed craft.

6. The box at the top of page 1 is for the builders' use. It is recommended that the identification number should be marked on all materials and equipment intended for incorporation in the craft.

7. If it is of great importance to the purchaser that the craft should be delivered by the date specified on schedule 3, then this section should be completed.

8 (a) Clause 3.3 to 3.6 is a price variation clause which allows the builders to adjust the price to reflect inflation occurring between the dates of the agreement and the final instalment falling due. The clause should be deleted where the parties agree on a "fixed-price contract", (usually where the period between signing and final payment is likely to be short).

(b) Builders are reminded that the clause does not permit a price increase to reflect inflation occurring between original quotation and signature of the agreement. For this reason builders should express their quotation as valid for a limited period and, if necessary, should revise them where the agreement is signed after that period.

(c) The clause allows builders to increase the price so as to reflect all increases in the Retail Prices Index occurring after the date of the agreement. If they intend to rely on the clause, builders should base the price on current costs without the addition of any inflation factor.

9. If the purchaser leaves or arranges for others to leave any item on the builders' premises or on the craft, he should insure the item himself unless the builders expressly agree in writing to do so. Builders should in any event carry adequate insurance cover against claims arising from their negligence which result in damage to any property on their premises.

10. Statutory Rights – Nothing in this agreement shall affect the consumer's statutory rights, which rights include conformity with any description or sample, satisfactory quality and fitness for any stated purpose.

11 Additional copies of this agreement may be obtained from

British Marine Federation,
Marine House,
Thorpe Lea Road,
Egham,
Surrey TW20 8BF.

or

Royal Yachting Association,
RYA House,
Ensign Way,
Hamble,
Hampshire SO31 4YA.

Appendix 2

Agreement for the Sale of a Second-hand Yacht

An agreement prepared by the Royal Yachting Association for the sale of a second-hand yacht between persons not normally engaged in the business of selling yachts.

AN AGREEMENT made the ___ day of ____ 20 ____

BETWEEN:

1 'The Vendor' :
of

2 'The Purchaser' :
of

The terms 'Vendor' and 'Purchaser' include their respective successors in title and the Vendor and Purchaser shall hereinafter be collectively referred to as 'the Parties'.

'The Purchase Price' : £_____sterling

'The Deposit' _____: 10% of the Purchase Price

In respect of the sale of a [REGISTERED/UNREGISTERED] PLEASURE CRAFT

Name :
Description :
Official No. :
Port of Registry where applicable :
Hull Identification Number:
Now lying at :

Including all equipment, machinery and gear on board ('the Yacht') and any specific inventory attached hereto initialled by the Parties and forming part of this Agreement.

1 Agreement for sale

The Vendor hereby agrees to sell and the Purchaser agrees to purchase the Yacht free from any encumbrances (subject to the conditions and terms of this agreement), together with all her outfit gear and equipment as set out in a schedule hereto but not including stores or the Vendor's personal effects, for the Purchase Price.

2 Payment of deposit

On the signing of this agreement the Deposit is to be paid to the Vendor and the balance of the Purchase Price together with any Value Added Tax shall be payable in accordance with Clause 6.

3.1 Value Added Tax

The Vendor [is/is not] a registered person for the purpose of the regulations relating to Value Added Tax and the Purchase Price [is/is not] exclusive of Value Added Tax.

3.2 Import dues and local taxes (craft lying overseas)

The Vendor warrants that the craft has been properly imported into [   ] and that all appropriate local taxes and dues have been paid and that the proposed sale is in accordance with all relevant local laws and regulations.

4 Inspection survey

The Purchaser may, at a venue to be agreed and at his own cost, haul out or place ashore and/or open up the Yacht and her machinery for the purposes of inspection and/or survey which, including any written report, shall be completed within [   ] days of the signing of this agreement. If any inspection requires more than superficial non-destructive dismantling the consent of the Vendor must be obtained before such work commences.

5.1 Notice of defects

Within fourteen days after completion of such inspection and/or survey if any material defect(s) in the Yacht or her machinery other than disclosed to the Purchaser in writing prior to the signing of this agreement or any material deficiencies in her inventory, if any, shall have been found the Purchaser may either :

5.1.1 give notice to the Vendor of his rejection of the Yacht provided that the notice shall specify any material defect(s) or deficiencies; or

5.1.2 give notice to the Vendor specifying any material defect(s) or deficiencies and requiring the Vendor forthwith either to make good the same or make a sufficient reduction in the Purchase Price to enable the Purchaser to make good the same. All agreed items of work to be completed without undue delay in all circumstances and to be carried out so as to satisfy the expressly specified requirements of the Purchaser's surveyor in respect only of material defects mentioned in his report and specified in the notice to the Vendor.

5.2 If the Purchaser shall have served a notice of rejection under Clause 5.1.1, then this agreement shall be deemed to be rescinded forthwith and the Vendor shall refund to the purchaser the Deposit in accordance with Clause 8.

5.3 If the Purchaser shall have served a notice under Clause 5.1.2 requiring the Vendor to make good material defects or deficiencies or to make a reduction in the Purchase Price, and the Vendor shall not have agreed within twenty one days after the service of the notice to make good such defects or the Parties have not agreed in the twenty one days after the service of notice upon the reduction in the Purchase Price, then this agreement shall be deemed to have been rescinded on the twenty second day after the service of notice and the Vendor shall refund to the Purchaser the Deposit in accordance with Clause 8.

In the case of any deficiencies in the Yacht's inventory (if any) remaining or arising within seven days of acceptance in accordance with Clause 6 the deficiencies shall be made good or a reduction in the Purchase Price shall be agreed, failing which this agreement shall be rescinded at the option of the Purchaser only.

6.1 Acceptance of yacht

The Yacht shall be deemed to have been accepted by the Purchaser and the balance of the Purchase Price and any Value Added Tax thereon shall become due and payable in accordance with Clause 7 upon the happening of any of the following events :

6.2 The expiry of fourteen days from the date of this agreement or such extended period as may be agreed between the Parties provided that no inspection or survey has been commenced;

6.3 The expiry of fifteen days from the completion of the survey, provided that the Purchaser has not served notice under Clause 5.1;

6.4 Notification in writing by the Vendor to the Purchaser of completion of the remedial works specified in a notice given by the Purchaser under Clause 5.1.2;

7.1 Completion of sale

Upon acceptance of the Yacht by the Purchaser, the Deposit shall be treated as part payment of the Purchase Price. Within seven days of acceptance the Purchaser shall pay the balance of the Purchase Price and any Value Added Tax thereon and the Vendor shall :
In the case of a registered yacht

7.1.1 *Registered yacht*

provide the Purchaser with the Certificate of Registry, correct and updated, together with any other

documents appertaining to the Yacht and shall execute a Bill of Sale, in the prescribed form, in favour of the Purchaser or his nominee, showing the Yacht to be free from encumbrances and completed so as to ensure transfer on the Register;

OR

7.1.2 *In the case of an unregistered yacht*

(including a yacht registered on the SSR)

(a) Provide the Purchaser with a Bill of Sale in favour of the Purchaser or his nominee, together with any other documents appertaining to the Yacht;

(b) Deliver to the Purchaser any necessary delivery order or other authority enabling the Purchaser to take immediate possession of the Yacht.

7.2 Where payment is made by cheque, draft, letter of credit or other instrument, the terms of this agreement shall not be deemed to have been fulfilled until such payment is cleared into the payee's account.

7.3 Vendor's right to assign title
By delivery of the documents specified in either case the Vendor shall be deemed to have covenanted AND HEREBY COVENANTS that he has the right to transfer property in the Yacht and that the same is free from all encumbrances, debts, liens and the like except such encumbrances and liabilities for duties, taxes, debts, liens and the like as are the responsibility of the Purchaser under Clauses 4 and 8.

7.4 Free access after completion
On completion, the Vendor shall ensure that

the Yacht is available for collection by the Purchaser and that free access by the Purchaser together with all necessary haulage equipment is permitted at no additional cost to the Purchaser.

8.1 Rescission of agreement

In the event of rescission of this agreement by the Purchaser he shall, at his own expense, reinstate the Yacht to the condition and position in which he found her, and shall pay all boatyard and surveyor's charges for this work.

8.2 Return of deposit

The Vendor shall thereupon return the Deposit to the Purchaser without deduction and without interest save that he shall be entitled to retain such part of the Deposit as shall be necessary to defray any boatyard or surveyor's charges not paid by the Purchaser.

Neither party shall thereafter have any claim against the other under this agreement.

9 Warranties

The Vendor being a person not selling the Yacht in the course of a business, and the Purchaser being at liberty to inspect the Yacht and satisfy himself as to her condition and specification, all express or implied warranties or conditions, statutory or otherwise, are hereby excluded and the Yacht, her outfit, gear and equipment shall be taken with all defects and faults of description without any allowance or abatement whatsoever.

10 Risk

Until the Yacht has been accepted or shall be deemed to have been accepted by the Purchaser she shall be at the risk of the Vendor who shall make good all damage sustained by her before the date of acceptance. If the Yacht be lost or becomes a constructive total loss before such acceptance, this agreement shall be null and void except that the Purchaser will be liable for the cost of all work authorised by him

under Clauses 4 and 8 and undertaken before such loss took place and the Deposit shall be returned to the Purchaser without interest but less any deduction made under Clauses 4 and 8 and otherwise without deduction and the Purchaser shall have no claim against the Vendor for damages or otherwise. After acceptance the Yacht shall in all respects be at the risk of the Purchaser.

Notwithstanding the provisions of this clause the ownership of the Yacht will not vest in the Purchaser until payment of the balance of the Purchase Price in accordance with Clause 7 even though the Purchaser may have insured his risk under the provisions of this clause.

11.1 Default by purchaser

Should the Purchaser fail to pay the balance of the Purchase Price in accordance with Clause 7, the Vendor may give notice in writing to the Purchaser requiring him to complete the purchase within fourteen days of the service of such notice.

If the Purchaser fails to comply with the notice then the Vendor may re-sell the Yacht by public auction or private treaty and any deposit paid shall thereupon be forfeit without prejudice to the Vendor's right to claim from the Purchaser the amount of any loss on re-sale together with all his reasonable costs and expenses, due allowance being made for any forfeited deposit. On the expiry of the said notice the Yacht shall be at the Vendor's risk.

11.2 Default by vendor

If the Vendor shall default in the execution of his part of the contract the Purchaser shall, without prejudice to any other rights he may have hereunder, be entitled to the return of the Deposit.

Unless such default by the Vendor shall have arisen from events over which the Vendor had no control, the Vendor shall pay interest upon the amount of the Deposit for the period during which he has held it at the rate of 4% per annum above finance house base rate, together with compensation for any loss which the Purchaser may have sustained as a result of the Vendor's default.

12 Arbitration

All disputes that cannot be resolved between the Parties and which arise out of or in connection with this agreement shall be submitted to a single arbitrator to be appointed, in default of agreement, by the Chairman of the Council of the RYA and the provisions of the Arbitration Act shall apply.

13 Notices

Any notice under this agreement shall be in writing and any notice to the Purchaser or Vendor shall be sufficiently served if delivered to him personally or posted by recorded delivery to his last known address. Any notice posted shall be deemed to have been received forty eight hours after the time of posting and any notice given in any other manner shall be deemed to have been received at the time when, in the ordinary course of post, it may be expected to have been received.

14 Jurisdiction

This agreement shall be construed according to, and governed by the Law of England (or of Scotland if the Vendor's address shall be in that country) and the Parties hereby submit

to the jurisdiction of the Courts of the same countries.

15 Marginal notes

The construction of this agreement is not to be affected by any marginal notes.

16 Rights under contract or statute

This agreement forms the entire agreement between the Parties unless otherwise specifically agreed in writing between them.

SIGNED BY THE VENDOR

In the presence of :

SIGNED BY THE PURCHASER

In the presence of :

Appendix 3

Agreement for the Syndicate Ownership of a Yacht

Agreement for the Syndicate Ownership of a Yacht

AN AGREEMENT made the   day of   20

BETWEEN   of
                    ("the first owner").
and   of
                    ("the second owner").

The owners include their respective successors in title and shall hereinafter be collectively referred to as "the Parties".

WHEREAS the Parties wish to enter into an agreement to share the management and use of the yacht "   " ("the Yacht")

[and **WHEREAS** the first owner is the present owner of the Yacht]

[and **WHEREAS** the second owner has by a prior contract purchased from the first owner   /64ths of the Yacht]

and **WHEREAS** the Parties have jointly and severally purchased the Yacht in the following shares :

   the first owner purchasing   /64ths

   the second owner purchasing   /64ths

[and **WHEREAS** the Parties have jointly and severally entered into an agreement with
[   ] (the "Mortgage Company")].

NOW IT IS HEREBY MUTUALLY AGREED between the Parties as follows :

1. Joint Bank Account

The first owner shall forthwith open a [Bank / Building Society] account ("the Account") in the names of the Parties into which the Parties shall upon the [   ] day of [   ] in each year transfer an amount of £[   ] until six months after the termination of this agreement in accordance with Clause 5.

2. Withdrawals and Contributions from/to Account

The first [and second] owner / s shall have power [jointly/ separately]to draw monies from the Account for the sole purpose of the maintenance and management of the Yacht as [he / they] shall in their absolute discretion think fit and shall have power to call for further and necessary contributions in equal shares from [the second owner / each other] subject always to the safeguards in Clause 4.7 and to the general law affecting principal and agent.

3. Casual Disbursements

Any disbursement, payment or account discharged by one owner on behalf of the other and of the general management of the Yacht shall from time to time as convenient but certainly once annually be reported to the other owner and each owner jointly and severally agrees to contribute one half of such disbursements, payments or accounts upon proper documentation in the form of receipts, etc. being presented as evidence of payment.

4. Management Responsibilities

The first owner shall have the following powers, duties and responsibilities :

4.1 to make day-to-day decisions for the general management of the Yacht;

4.2 to make (after consultation with the second owner) any arrangement for the purchase of capital equipment such as sails, engines, etc. as may be necessary and for any agreement to charter the Yacht;

4.3 to insure the Yacht, her apparel, fittings etc. against the usual risks either at Lloyds or with an insurance company or association;

4.4 to employ any yard, sail-loft, brokers or agents on their usual terms of business and to transact any necessary business in relation to the Yacht;

4.5 to make, adjust, apportion or settle at his discretion any salvage, damage, average or other claims in favour of or against the Yacht or to refer the same to arbitration;

4.6 to take such steps as may be necessary to defend proceedings, accept service or arrange finance relating to the Yacht;

4.7 as soon as reasonably practicable after the [   ] day of [   ] in each year to render to the second owner accounts paid together with the Account statements as evidence of payment, and on request to produce all vouchers, books or other documents and papers relating to the management of the Account and of the Yacht.

5 Termination of Agreement

If either of the Parties has reasonable cause or desire to terminate this agreement, he may, by individual notice in writing to the other party, indicate his desire to terminate. Such termination shall take place within six months after the delivery of such notice in writing.

Upon such notice in writing being delivered, the other party shall take such steps as may be necessary to secure the execution of a proper release and indemnity against all liabilities contracted by the determining party and shall arrange to purchase the share of the determining party at a fair market price or alternatively obtain agreement by another to take on the share of the determining party. Likewise, the settle all his share of the disbursements, payments or accounts for maintenance of the Yacht up to and including the date of actual termination as agreed between the Parties which for the avoidance of doubt may be any date within six months of the individual notice in writing being received by the other party.

If a dispute arises as to the price to be paid to the determining party for his share then a valuation shall be obtained from a recognised yacht broker and in default of agreement the entirely of the Yacht shall be publicly advertised for sale with notice of time and place for sale being given to both Parties and she shall be sold. Each of the Parties on receiving his share of the purchase money shall execute the necessary Bill of Sale of his share in the Yacht of the purchaser and deliver up possession of the Yacht. The costs of such sale shall be paid by the Parties according to their respective shares.

6. Where it is agreed to terminate this agreement and the Parties have mutually agreed to sell the Yacht, it shall then be sold either by private treaty at such price as the Parties may agree or, in default of such agreement, by public auction subject to such conditions as are usual on the sale of such yachts. Each of the Parties shall be at liberty to bid for and purchase the Yacht at any such public auction, or to purchase the Yacht outright for the price advertised for sale by private treaty.

7.1 Regular payment of mortgage etc

[In the case of a mortgage or hire purchase agreement being in operation each owner jointly and severally agrees to pay his monthly or other contribution to defray the costs of such mortgage or hire purchase agreement

into the Account in accordance with Clause 1 until the date of determination agreed in accordance with Clause 5.

7.2 Final settlement of Mortgage debt

In the event of the sale of the Yacht, each owner jointly and severally agrees with the other to defray from his share of the sale price his share settlement of the mortgage or hire purchase agreement entered into with the Mortgage Company.]

8. If any dispute, difference or question arises between the Parties relating to the rights, duties or obligations of either of them, including (without prejudice to the generality hereof) any dispute, difference or question whether the owners have, in fact, properly and satisfactorily carried out their obligations under this agreement, the same shall be referred to arbitration by a single arbitrator to be agreed upon by the Parties or, failing such agreement, appointed by the Secretary-General of the RYA. This shall be deemed to be a submission to arbitration within the Arbitration Act 1950.

9. Any notice under this agreement shall be in writing and shall be sufficiently served if delivered personally or posted to the last known postal address in Great Britain or Ireland of either of the Parties.

IN WITNESS whereof this agreement has been signed by the Parties the day and the year first above written

SIGNED BY THE FIRST OWNER... in presence of :

SIGNED BY THE SECOND OWNER... in the presence of:

Appendix 4

RYA Bill of Sale for Private Transactions

BILL OF SALE

FOR THE YACHT '...' ('the Yacht')
Type: ....
Year Built: ....
Length: ....
Beam: ....
Auxiliary Power: ....
Small Ships Register No: ....

I/We
.... [and ....
of: .... of: ....
....]

('the Transferor[s]')

IN CONSIDERATION of the sum of £.........................
(..pounds) paid to me/us by:

.... [and ....
of: .... of: ....
....]

('the Transferee[s]')

receipt of which is acknowledged;

1.   transfer the Yacht to the Transferee[s];
2.   for myself/ourselves and for my/our heirs covenant with the Transferees and
      his/their heirs and assigns that I/we have power so to transfer and that the
      Yacht is free from encumbrances.

SIGNED this ....day of...20[   ]

.... (signature of Transferor[s])
[...]

in the presence of:

.... (signature of Witness)
.... (name of Witness)
of: .... (address of Witness)

Notes:
1. This form of Bill of Sale is produced by the RYA for use by personal members on the transfer of an unregistered yacht or a yacht registered on the Small Ships Register. Transfers of yachts registered under Part I of the 1995 Merchant Shipping Act should be evidenced using the Bill of Sale prescribed by The Registry of Shipping and Seamen, PO Box 420, Cardiff. CF24 5XR.
2. Please delete inapplicable alternatives.
This form of Bill of Sale should not be used if any of the parties to it is a corporate body.

A simple Bill of Sale for use between a private buyer and a private seller of a sailing cruiser not on the Part I Register of British Ships

Appendix 5

VAT Guide for Yachts
isssued by HM Customs and Excise

(Not including Channel Islands, Malta or Gibraltar)

This leaflet is for UK yachtsmen who still have concerns about VAT when cruising in the EC or when returning from outside the EC.

VESSELS PURCHASED/ACQUIRED WITHIN THE EC

UK residents should only use a boat in the Community if it is VAT paid, or 'deemed' VAT paid. Documentary evidence supporting this should be carried at all times.

- Original invoice or receipt
- Evidence that VAT was paid at importation

If the vessel was in use as a private pleasure craft before 1/1/1985 and was in the EC on 31/12/1992, it may be 'deemed' VAT paid under an age-related relief. Documentary evidence to support this could be:

For Age

- Marine Survey
- Part 1 Registration
- Insurance Documents
- Builders Certificate

For Location at 31/12/92

- Receipt for mooring
- Receipt for Harbour Dues
- Dry dock records

As Austria, Finland and Sweden joined the Single Market two years later, the relevant dates will be .... in use before 1/1/1987 and moored in EC on 31/12/1994.

Other documents which could demonstrate VAT status could be:

- Evidence that Returned Goods Relief (RGR) has been granted
- Evidence that Transfer of Residence Relief (TOR) has been granted (Subject to one year restriction on disposal).

In the absence of any of the above, whilst cruising within the EC you should carry a Bill of Sale (between two private individuals in the UK). Whilst this is not conclusive proof that VAT has been paid, it does indicate that tax status is the responsibility of UK Customs.

VESSELS PURCHASED/ACQUIRED OUTSIDE THE EC

ANY yacht purchased outside the EC will be liable for VAT, regardless of age or previous tax history. There may also be Import Duty unless the vessel is more than 12m overall or built in the EC. Charges become due at the first port of call within the EC (See Public Notice No 3).

BUYING A NEW VESSEL IN ONE MEMBER STATE OF THE EC TO TAKE TO ANOTHER

Yachts purchased NEW within the EC pay VAT at the country of destination. For example, if you buy a new yacht in France, you should send appendix D of Public Notice No 728 to the Personal Transport Unit (address below) within 7 days of arrival in the UK.

BUYING A VESSEL IN THE UK FOR EXPORT FROM THE EC

You can purchase a vessel tax free if you intend to export it, under its own power to a destination outside the EC. Full details can be found in VAT leaflet 703/3/98.

VOYAGES OUTSIDE THE EC

Part 1 of form C1331 should be lodged with Customs prior to departure if you are going directly to a country outside the EC, ie Channel Islands, Malta and Gibraltar etc.
On return to the UK you should report your arrival as per Public Notice No. 8 page 6.

For further information contact your local Advice Centre, or look in your phone book under Customs & Excise.
This information sheet is produced by the National Unit for Personal Transport (PTU) HM Customs & Excise (MSO), PO Box 242, Dover CT17 9GP.

Appendix 6

EU Recreational Craft Directive

Importing of a second-hand boat into the European Economic Area and boats built for own use

General
Since 16 June 1998 all recreational craft, with few exceptions, between 2.5m and 24m in length, imported into the EEA for the first time, and home-built boats if placed on the market within five years of completion, must comply with the essential requirements of the RCD and must be CE marked to certify this compliance. The builder, his agent or the person importing the boat is responsible for such compliance and marking.

Application
The European Economic Area (EEA) includes all EU countries and their dependent territories plus Iceland and Norway.
Put into service means the first use by the end user but does not include boats temporarily put into service for reasons of tourism or transit.
Placing on the market means the first making available against payment or free of charge.

Boats that will need to comply with the Directive and be CE marked
These include:

• Boats built outside the EEA which were not put into service in the EEA prior to 16 June 1998.
• Boats built for own use if subsequently placed on the EEA market during a period of five years of completion.

Boats that will not need to comply with the Directive

These include:

- Boats completed or put into service in the EEA prior to 16 June 1998.
- Boats built in the EEA prior to 16 June 1998 even if exported and subsequently re-imported after 16 June 1998.
- Boats built for own use provided they are not subsequently placed on the EEA market during a period of five years.
- Boats intended for racing and labelled as such by the manufacturer, his agent or the importer.
- Canoes, kayaks, gondolas, pedalos, sailing surfboards, powered surfboards and personal watercraft.
- Boats designed before 1950, built predominantly of the original materials and labelled as such by the manufacturer, his agent or the importer.
- All boats entering the EEA for reasons of tourism or in transit.

Should you be in any doubt whatsoever about whether or not your boat needs to comply then contact the RYA.

Please consider this carefully as should your boat need to comply and you fail to ensure this you may be subject to three months imprisonment and/or £5,000 fine.

Compliance with the Directive

Should your boat need to comply with the Directive the RYA can help by supplying further information on correct compliance. Contact the RYA Technical Unit.

Appendix 7

RYA Courses, Books and Useful Addresses

We are fortunate in this country (so far) in having no heavy-handed bureaucracy that requires those of us who go to sea for recreation to apply for pieces of paper to permit us to do so, or pass tests to prove our competence. There are many who think the coming of such a day to be only a matter of time – happily, it has been 'only a matter of time' now for many years. There is no doubt that the greatest bulwark against such an encroachment on our personal freedoms is the demonstration that those of us who go to sea for recreation do not need such regulation because we regulate ourselves. 'Education, not legislation' has been the RYA's mantra since the 1960s, and in putting that mantra into practice the RYA has, in concert with government departments who might otherwise take on the task for themselves, developed a matrix of training schemes and associated qualifications which have been copied all over the world.

Before actually buying your first sailing cruiser, you should have gained the knowledge and experience to take her out without being a danger to yourself, your family, other seafarers and the rescue services. You may have gained this knowledge through crewing and learning with friends, through sailing dinghies before taking to bigger boats, or through attending an RYA-recognised sailing school and undertaking and passing at least some of the training courses available.

At the very least, you should already have passed, or have the knowledge and experience to pass, the RYA's Day Skipper course – the very basic level of knowledge, without which, taking a small boat to sea is simply irresponsible and potentially downright dangerous. Just as much to the point, you may not actually get the boat to sea.

The Day Skipper Certificate really is the simple basics; Coastal Skipper, the next highest qualification, will open up to you the things you need to know even for simple estuary cruising, and in particular, if you plan to do the sort of cruising that might keep you out after dark. You will also find that many charter companies and holiday operators will ask for at least Coastal Skipper from whomsoever is to be in charge of any sailing cruiser you wish to charter while on holiday.

The standard qualification for any self-respecting sailing cruiser owner is the RYA Yachtmaster Offshore certificate. To hold it, you must attend, and pass, the shore-based theory course (navigation, regulations, meteorology – things like that) and have spent the time at sea necessary to give you the experience that can simply not be acquired by just taking a 5- or even 10-day course. To gain the certificate you must pass a Direct Entry Examination, usually conducted in your own boat by an RYA-appointed examiner. No one suggests – least of all the RYA – that holding a Yachtmaster ticket 'proves' you are qualified in all respects to go to sea but everyone knows that you cannot get one without having demonstrated sailing competence and at least some level of understanding of the many things the sea will surely demand of you.

RYA National Cruising Scheme

Course	Minimum experience	Assumed knowledge	Course content	Ability after course	Minimum duration
Competent Crew Practical	None	None	Basic seamanship and steering	Useful crew member	5 days
Day Skipper Shorebased	Some practical experience desirable	None	Basic seamanship, introduction to navigation and meteorology		Can be taken over a winter one evening a week at evening class
Day Skipper Practical	5 days; 100 miles; 4 night hours	Basic navigation and sailing ability	Basic pilotage, boat handling, seamanship and navigation	Skipper a small yacht in familiar waters by day	5 days
Diesel engine course	None	None	Diesel engine operation, maintenance and simple defect rectification	Operate a diesel engine effectively and carry out simple repairs	6 hours
Coastal Skipper Yachtmaster Shorebased		Navigation to Day Skipper shorebased standard	Offshore and coastal navigation, pilotage, meteorology		
Coastal Skipper Practical	15 days (2 as skipper); 300 miles; 8 night hours	Navigation to Coastal Skipper shorebased standard. Sailing to Day Skipper standard	Skipper techniques for coastal and offshore passages	Skipper a yacht on coastal passages by day and night	5 days
Yachtmaster Ocean Shorebased	Coastal and offshore passages	Navigation to Coastal Skipper and Yachtmaster offshore standard	Astro-navigation, ocean meteorology, passage planning		

Examination RYA/DoT Certificates of Competence

Grade of examination	Minimum sea time within 10 yrs of examination	Certificates required before examination
RYA/DoT Coastal Skipper	30 days 2 as skipper; 800 miles; 12 night hours	Restricted (VHF) Radio Operator; First Aid
RYA/DoT Yachtmaster	50 days; 2,500 miles; 5 days as skipper; 5 passages over 60 miles, including 2 overnight and 2 as skipper	Restricted (VHF) Radio Operator; First Aid
RYA/DoT Yachtmaster Ocean	Ocean passage as skipper or mate of watch	RYA/DoT Yachtmaster Offshore certificate and Yachtmaster Ocean Shorebased Course

RYA publications

Something over 70% of the 80,000-plus people who are personal members of the RYA give cruising under sail or under power as their principal boating activity – so when you join you will be in good company. As a personal member you will be entitled to some of the RYA's many information booklets for free, as part of your annual subscription, or you can get a discount off the publisher's price of some others. The RYA catalogue lists some 200 titles, including many written by the RYA's own experts specifically for members who cruise under sail. Among these are the following, plus the titles listed on page ii of this book.

Planning a Foreign Cruise – two booklets giving rules and regulations which apply to visiting cruising sailors in all the countries of the Baltic, North Sea and Atlantic coast of Europe including UK, Ireland, Channel Isles, Faeroes, Iceland and the Mediterranean.

Weather Forecasts – where to find them, how to use them.

RYA Met Map Pads – 40 maps and pads (for use with radio shipping forecasts) bound in a booklet.

Cruising Yacht Safety – safety recommendations categorised according to type of craft.

Collision Regulations – the International Regulations for the Avoidance of Collision at Sea (the ColRegs, as they are known) annotated and illustrated for cruising sailors.

Marina Guide – Prices and facilities at over 150 coastal and 100 inland marinas in the UK, plus 30 in France.

The Yachtsman's Lawyer – a comprehensive guide to the law for individual yachtsmen.

Cruising Logbook – personal log and syllabus for Yachtmaster, Coastal and Day Skipper courses, as well as Competent Crew.

Adlard Coles Nautical also publishes the following books in *The RYA Book of* **series:**

The RYA Book of Navigation 2nd edition by Tim Bartlett, ISBN 0-7136-6322-7

The Adlard Coles Book of Navigation Exercises by Alison Noice and James Stevens, ISBN 0-7136-6323-5

The RYA Book of Knots by Peter Owen, ISBN 0-7136-5898-3

The RYA Book of the International Certificate of Competence by Bill Anderson, ISBN 0-7136-6248-4

The RYA Book of Diesel Engines 2nd edition by Tim Bartlett, ISBN 0-7136-6358-8

The RYA Book of Outboard Motors 2nd edition by Tim Bartlett, ISBN 0-7136-6873-3

The RYA Book of Buying Your First Motor Cruiser by Robert Avis, ISBN 0-7136-5074-5

The Adlard Coles Book of EuroRegs for Inland Waterways by Marian Martin, ISBN 0-7136-6589-0

The RYA Book of Caribbean Cruising by Jane Gibb, ISBN 0-7136-5431-7

The RYA Book of Mediterranean Cruising by Rod Heikell, ISBN 0-7136-5808-8

The RYA Book of Race Training by Jim Saltonstall, ISBN 0-7136-4284-X

Useful addresses and telephone numbers

Royal Yachting Association
RYA House,
Ensign Way,
Hamble,
Hampshire SO31 4YA
Tel: 01703 627400

British Marine Federation
Meadlake Place,
Thorpe Lea Road,
Egham,
Surrey
TW20 8HE
Tel: 01784 473377

Registry of Shipping and Seamen
PO Box 420,
Cardiff CF29 5XR
Tel: 02920 448800

Association of Brokers and Yacht Agents
Wheel House, Petersfield Road,
Whitehill, Borden,
Hampshire
GU35 9BU
Tel: 0845 900162
www.yodsa.co.uk

HM Customs and Excise
Dorset House,
Stamford Street,
London SE1 9PS
Tel: 0845 010 9000
www.hmce.gov.uk

Bishop Skinner & Co Ltd
(Insurance Brokers)
5 Oakley Crescent,
City Road,
London EC1V 1NU
Tel: 0800 783 80

103

Index